Integrity in Homemaking

Affirming the choice to be
a mother-at-home

Connie Fourré Zimney

Ave Maria Press   Notre Dame, Indiana

Library of Congress Catalog Card Number: 84-71285

International Standard Book Number: 0-87793-322-7

Cover and text design: Elizabeth French

Photography:
Robert J. Cunningham, 36, 82; William Koechling, 110; John and Cindy Stewart, 14; Strix Pix, 130; Paul Tucker, 52; Jim Whitmer, cover, 6.

Printed and bound in the United States of America.

Connie Fourré Zimney is a college graduate, a former high school teacher, and now an author. She is active in church life and has conducted workshops on Christian Homemaking. She *makes her home* in Hamel, Minnesota, with her husband and four small children.

Contents

Introduction

During my first pregnancy I looked forward to motherhood with alternating euphoria and panic. When I was feeling optimistic, I would imagine myself seated peacefully on the sofa, sunlight streaming through the window as I stitched away at a needlepoint project, my immaculate baby playing contentedly at my feet.

On blacker days I pictured myself pacing the floor with a screaming infant, my mounting frustration equalled only by my boredom. Secretly I was afraid that after a few months I would get tired of my baby and want to give him back—and there would be no one to take him.

Every mother knows there is truth in both visions. Whether we are parents of preschoolers or young adults, there are some days when we feel like exploding with the joy of seeing our children grow, and other times when we would like to shoot anything that moves. Being a parent seems to call forth the best and the worst in us; I have never loved a job so intensely—nor hated it so thoroughly—in my life.

Child Care, House Care

Ask someone to describe a good parent, and the list is likely to look something like this: nurturing, consistent disciplinarian, good listener, lively sense of humor. You are not likely to find, "wipes up spills immediately," or "is able to remove spots from any fabric." We have become highly aware of the importance of personal relationships and communication, and our thinking on parenting reflects this concern. Women who choose to stay home full time with their children expect to use their time to talk with their youngsters, applauding their achievements and consoling them with their problems. Many mothers of schoolchildren shun full-time jobs because they want to be available to their children for those after-school conversations.

Essential as communication is to a full human life, any mother who looks realistically at herself knows that the majority of her time is not spent in conversation, nor in relating directly to her family at all. Unless she has a houseful of servants, it is spent in such mundane tasks as cleaning, cooking and laundry. Recent studies indicate that the average family spends just minutes per week in meaningful conversation.

Most of us can take occasional satisfaction in a row of sweet-smelling, freshly ironed shirts or a newly waxed floor, but it is a rare person who truly enjoys the day-to-day reality of housework. I decided to stay home after the birth of our first child because I wanted to be with him, but as more children arrived in rapid succession the mounting housework seemed to take over my life. There were days when all I said to the children was, "Not now, I'm busy," or worse, "Go away and leave me alone!" My time and energy seemed to be eaten up by trivialities. As I mopped up spilled milk and swept up broken glasses, I would ask myself, "What am I doing here?"

But as time went on, I began to wonder whether there was more to cleaning closets and baking bread than I realized. I couldn't believe that the few moments I spent each day talking to my children about something significant, like cooperation, or God's love for us, were the only important times of the day. God would not create us in such a way that most of our time was simply wasted. Perhaps my sole purpose for being home was not face-to-face encounter with my children; perhaps my cooking and cleaning had a deeper purpose that I didn't yet understand.

All the home management books I've read are written about efficiency—not philosophy. The popular women's magazines are filled with articles on cooking and decorating, but those pages deal with the how—not the why. I wanted to understand more clearly what constituted a home and why it was important. When I began to ask myself the *why* behind my housekeeping, I went to my usual source of information: the library. There were no entries under *Homemaking*. The card file said simply "Homemaking—see Home Economics." I felt certain that books on home economics would not answer the questions I was asking.

Lack of Preparation

It seems that we enter most jobs with some idea of what we are about. Homemaking is a job which most of us begin without much preparation. Many of us have spent years in school preparing for other careers. Even those who take a job without any previous training generally get on-the-job instruction from their employers. But homemakers step through the door, usually with a new baby and a lot of good wishes, and then we're on our own.

Some women start out homemaking with nothing but courage and a sense of humor, and somehow they survive. Most of us, however, picked up some homemaking skills from our mothers. I learned to cook and sew when I was growing up, although my cleaning is a little haphazard. Yet we have probably never discussed our goals as homemakers with our mothers. We rely on some sort of instinctive drive to set our housekeeping standards and the tempo of life at home, but it seems we should be able to come up with something better than instinct to guide us in a work that will consume a good portion of our lives.

Much of our schooling is actually counterproductive to successful homemaking. Never once, in all my years of education, do I recall a discussion of physical work. From an academic point of view, physical work hardly seems to exist. We are trained to challenge our minds, and then suddenly we are thrown into a situation where our intellectual achievements become almost irrelevant. I left teaching high school, for which

I was trained and in which I felt competent, and went into homemaking, where I constantly felt incompetent at jobs which a child could be trained to do.

In school, every test I ever took was administered in a silent room. To prepare people for homemaking, classrooms and libraries should be staffed with two or three people who tug on students' elbows and interrupt their work at three-minute intervals.

Most schools—and jobs—are geared toward achievement. Successful students complete their tasks and are rewarded with high grades, honors and scholarships. Successful workers receive promotions, praise and raises. There are no honors, promotions or raises for the homemaker. An achievement-oriented homemaker has nothing to point to: the better her cake, the faster it will disappear, and the more highly polished the coffee table, the more obvious will be those first fingerprints.

And always, homemakers, whether part time or full time, face a dilemma. Besides our important task of mothering, we still have housework to do. Whatever our skills in cooking and cleaning, we will probably find that housework demands more time than we would like, and that the work itself can be discouraging. The underlying importance and dignity of our work has not been made clear. We know *how*, but we don't always know *why*.

Toward a Solution

The homemaker will be offered some stock solutions to the problem of housework. A sympathetic relative or friend will suggest getting away from things for a while. Hiring a babysitter and spending an afternoon on the town can give the frazzled homemaker a new lease on life. In cases where it is financially feasible, hiring help can offer some relief. Undoubtedly someone will suggest finding a job away from home!

An important change in recent years is that many husbands are beginning to share the housework. Furthermore, an entire industry has been built up for the purpose of reducing housework. From instant muffins to vacuum cleaners, our stores and homes are filled with products which lighten our load.

Whether we reduce our workload with appliances, or share it with a husband or hired help, or just escape from it occasionally, we have still achieved only a partial solution. Unless we hire a full-time household staff, we will still have housework to do. Treating that housework as merely a necessary evil robs us of the satisfaction we need and deserve.

A More Fundamental Solution

Besides increasing our efficiency and sharing our responsibilities, it is important for us to appreciate the significance of our work. God's will for us may well be revealed through the needs of the people around us. We all have an innate need for some sort of home, and it is God's will that we as parents provide that home for our children. Whether that effort requires a full-time or part-time commitment calls for individual discernment, but in either case a better understanding of our work will promote more effective homemaking.

Introduction

The word *vocation* used to call to mind a commitment to the priesthood or the religious life. But now we understand that each of us has a vocation, or calling from God, and for many of us that vocation is homemaking.

The church has developed all sorts of theologies: We have a theology of priesthood, a theology of marriage, a theology of liberation, a theology of work. The many different religious orders in the world have well-defined goals and spiritualities. And yet, in spite of the fact that millions of women throughout the centuries have been called to a life of homemaking, I have never heard of a theology of homemaking. If theology is "faith seeking understanding," then our attempts to discover the purpose in our vocation is indeed the beginning of a theology of homemaking. An important part of attaining serenity as homemakers is an ability to see God's hand in our lives, and to feel confident of his plan for us.

We also need the confidence that comes from knowing we are making a significant contribution to the well-being of our families and of society. It is important for us to clarify our goals and to re-examine the means for achieving them. We need a grasp on what is truly essential about homemaking, so we can use our time most effectively.

The first step toward establishing our goals is to understand what precisely we mean when we talk about *home*. For the purposes of this book, we will define home as *a geographical place in which a group of people spend time together in such a way that their common life binds them together and both expresses and fosters their values.* That is, home = people + place + time ⟶ love + values fostered + values expressed.

In *In Praise of Homemaking* we will explore our role as home*makers,* and we will examine the three elements—people, place and time—listed above.

The homemaker will be referred to as *she* throughout because most homemakers today are women; this is not to deny the important contribution of men to homemaking. I will be speaking out of my own experience as a full-time homemaker with young children, but it is my hope that all homemakers, male and female, full time, part time or past time, will see themselves in these pages as I attempt to articulate the special challenge that is homemaking.

Occupation?

Shortly before our first child was born, I decided to take out a library card. I had just quit my job and was sure I would have plenty of time for reading now that I was home all day. It was a glorious autumn day, perfect for a stroll, so I waddled happily over to our old brick library and picked up an application. I carefully wrote in my name, address and phone number as asked, but the last question on the form took me by surprise. For some reason the library wanted to know my occupation.

"I'm not a teacher anymore," I thought. "I don't *have* an occupation. I'm not anything!" I stared blankly at the application for a few more minutes and then sheepishly handed it back to the librarian with the final question unanswered. I felt embarrassed to be so obviously pregnant and yet so apparently without legitimate means of support.

Later, of course, I realized that the expected answer was *housewife.* Up until that time housewives had always been other women, and it hadn't yet occurred to me that I had finally joined their ranks. This was the first time after leaving teaching that I had been asked to label my new occupation, and that afternoon at the library was just the first step in a long effort to understand my new role.

Mother? Housewife? Homemaker?

For a time, when someone asked my occupation I replied that I was a full-time mother, but something about that answer made me uncomfortable. My husband is a father, yet that's never been his response when questioned about his occupation. And what about mothers working outside the home? If I am a full-time mother, does that make them part-time mothers? Women with grown children are mothers, yet mothering takes a very small percentage of their time. Those people are parents just as truly as I am, but we do not share the same occupation.

Wife and *mother* are words that describe relationships, not occupations. Women tend to define themselves in terms of relationships: We are someone's wife, someone's mother, or someone's daughter. The result is that we become overly dependent on those people. In a sense, if those people disappear from our lives, we cease to exist. A woman who sees herself primarily as a mother may find herself floundering when her children leave home. With so little expected of her as a mother, she feels as though her very self has left home along with her children.

I am a wife and mother, and those relationships are central to my life. They are the source of my most intense joy as well as moments of aching sorrow. Although I choose to stay home because of my hus-

band and children, those relationships still do not con-
stitute my occupation.

After deciding that mother wasn't the best way to
describe myself, I called myself a housewife for a
while, but only when hard pressed. The term isn't
really inaccurate, just incomplete. It connotes only the
physical aspects of my job such as taking care of a
house, managing money, keeping things tidy, putting
meals on the table at fairly predictable hours. It
doesn't consider the relationship at all.

A more adequate term is *homemaker*. At first I
felt that saying I was a homemaker was a little preten-
tious, like trying to dress things up so they would look
better. However, the longer I reflected on my role,
the more fitting the title seemed. With other homemakers I share the privilege of *shaping the living environments of those we serve*. The tasks that fill my
days are really done for the purpose of making our
house a home for my family.

Homemaking is a job, as farming or woodwork-
ing are jobs. I do not just live in relation to my husband and children; I have a task to perform just as
other workers do. A farmer produces food, a cabinetmaker crafts furniture, and I make a home. My decision to stay home would make no sense if it were not
for my husband and children, but by the same token it
would be pointless for a farmer to grow tomatoes if
there were no one to eat them, and there would be no
reason for a cabinetmaker to make a chair if there
were no one to sit on it.

Even before sweet corn is harvested or the legs
are glued on a table, their producers enjoy moments

of satisfaction in their work. A farmer rejoices in the neat rows of corn as they sprout, long before they become food. A woodworker is pleased with a nicely turned edge before he even attempts to fit the pieces of wood together. Those workers take pleasure in a fine piece of work, and a homemaker also can be proud of the home she creates.

It is especially important for us to be able to see the value of our job during times of stress in our families. Adolescents often go through a stage of challenging their parents and rejecting their homes, and homemakers can wonder whether their years of service have been wasted.

In such a situation, a homemaker is like an architect who designs a building that is ahead of its time. The building may be a fine example of design, but people who are not ready for it are unable to appreciate it. There is always hope that an architect's talent may be recognized. And teen-agers usually do grow past their rebellious years and come back as adults to enjoy the special character of their homes. We always hope for recognition for creating something which is less tangible but no less real than a church building. Even, and perhaps especially, if some of our family relationships break down, we need to take pride in the truth and beauty we instilled in our homes, imperfect though our efforts may have been.

Is Homemaking a Profession?

Once I decided on homemaker as a name for my career, I began to wonder where homemaking fit in relation to other occupations. As a teacher I had been a professional. I took pride in my training and my work, and as a homemaker I wanted to be proud of my new job. When I reflected on my career I wondered, "Am I still a professional? Is homemaking a profession?"

I realized that I wasn't exactly sure what was meant by the term *professional.* I consulted a dictionary, but was disappointed at what I discovered. A profession is "an occupation or vocation requiring training . . . and advanced study in a specialized field."

I used to be a professional, all right, but apparently that's in the past. "Training" could be helpful and "advanced study" might make us more creative and interesting, but neither is on anybody's list of requirements. As homemakers we are not professionals.

Homemakers Are Artists

When I discovered I was no longer a practicing professional, I looked for some other occupational category. It occurred to me that artists are notorious for working unrecognized and underpaid; perhaps I was engaging in an art. I flipped the dictionary open to the entry for *art,* and there I saw myself. According to the dictionary, an art is "a form of human activity appealing to the imagination . . . a skill." A good homemaker is a highly-skilled person, with competence in food preparation, money management, interior decoration, and many other areas. Even more important, she is a person of imagination. Few of us are completely satisfied with our homes as they are. We would always like to find a way to make the hamburger less boring or the living room more inviting. An effective homemaker imaginatively finds new possibilities for her family and creates strategies for achieving them.

The more I considered the notion of myself as an artist, the better I liked it. An artist is a person who takes some raw materials, such as watercolors or clay, and creates something new and beautiful out of them. Without the hand of the artist, potters' clay is just a brown lump. It does not catch the eye, it communicates nothing, it has little beauty. The artist transforms this lifeless mass into something capable of making a statement and touching the heart.

Homemakers are artists, but instead of working in paint or metal we work with people, places and time. We have a small group of people to work with: our husband, our children, perhaps members of our extended family. We have a place: a rambling old farmhouse, a three-bedroom ranch, a small apartment in the heart of the city, or a few rooms in someone else's house. And we have time: birthdays, holidays, shimmering summer afternoons, dreary March mornings when the clouds seem never to lift. As artists, it is our job to take these elements and shape them into a home that warms us and witnesses to the deepest truths in our lives.

Not every combination of persons, places and time results in a home. A factory, too, has people spending time together in a given place. Factory workers even share a common goal of production, but a factory is certainly not a home. We don't go to the assembly line for comfort, for relaxation, or to share a victory. We spend the really special moments in our homes.

Unless there is someone who consciously shapes the elements, the important people at our house can simply jostle along from day to day. In the absence of a strong home life, parents and children begin to look outside the family for understanding and support. Neglected, a house becomes more and more unkempt, a place to escape from rather than relax in. Precious days slip by unnoticed until suddenly children are grown up and gone, and husband and wife discover they have become strangers.

All of us are occasionally struck with the awful thought: What would happen to our families if we were no longer there? We know that somehow the children would be fed and the laundry tended. A housekeeper could take care of the physical needs of the family, but she could not supply the heart. The homemaker is the person who creates the birthday parties and decorates the house for Christmas. Without us our house might take on the sterility of an assembly line or the bright chaos of a college dormitory; but it would no longer have the fullness of a complete home life which we bring.

The Artist's Vision

We have spoken of the raw materials which artists use to produce their works, but there is another essential element that we have not yet mentioned: the artist's vision. Not everyone can take a palette of oil paints or a box of pastel chalk and do something worthwhile with them. The true artist has an image within her which she somehow translates into concrete reality through the materials she works with.

Imagine for a moment that I asked you to sketch a horse. Your first reaction might be to protest that drawing horses isn't one of your talents, but suppose you agreed to try. You probably would not begin to draw the minute you had paper and pencil in hand. First you would try to remember what a horse looks like—*really* looks like. You would think for a minute about the proportions of a horse: How big is the head in relation to the body, and how long should the legs be? Then you might begin to sketch a rough outline of the horse, trying for the general impression of the animal before tackling details. Or, you might decide to begin with one section of your drawing, working on defining the head of the horse, before worrying about the rest of the body. Chances are that after a few minutes of sketching something would start to look wrong. The neck would not be arching properly, or there would be something stiff about the shoulders. The drawing taking shape under your fingers would not quite match up with the vision in your head. You would become caught up in the lines you were putting to paper and lose touch with your vision.

It would be time for you to stop and take a minute to recapture the image you began with. You would look at your half-drawn sketch, then away, try-ing to remember the precise shape you wanted to create. After you had recollected your vision, you would bend back to work until you again became dissatisfied with your progress. It would be time for another break, and this process of alternating work with recapturing the image would continue until the sketch was complete.

The artist translates her vision from her imagination, through her hands, to the experience of another. It is a complex and fragile process which requires that she be able to hold fast to a mental image and to make her hands obey her mind in shaping that image. We homemaker/artists share the same process. Deep within us we have a vision of the home we would like to have, and we must constantly clarify and redefine that image as we bring it to life around us.

If you were asked to describe what comes to mind when the word *home* is mentioned, you would probably express both emotions and visual images. The picture that flashes into my mind when I think of home is of a little house at night, the soft glow from its windows shining on the deep snow covering the surrounding countryside. Immediately after that clear picture, all sorts of ideas come tumbling: security, sunshine, comfort, nurturing, growth.

Each of us has a different image of the home we would like for ourselves and our families. Our vision is made up of a combination of the good things we experienced in our homes growing up, bits and pieces we've seen of other people's homes, and some elements that spring from longings unique to us.

Homemakers share the struggle of the artist

drawing a horse. We have our vision, which is more or less clear to us, and we set about bringing that vision to life. Our idea of home influences whether we paint our kitchen cabinets a clear yellow or a somber blue and whether our family makes decisions democratically or autocratically. Like every other artist, we need to sharpen our image by becoming more and more certain of each detail, or we will lose it as we begin to work with our physical materials. One of the purposes of this book is to help us clarify our goals so we become more capable of achieving them.

Like the artist with the horse, we also can be hard at work when we begin to get the uneasy feeling that something is wrong. The new puppy I thought would bring some excitement to the household is causing chaos instead. The prayer time I instituted so heroically is provoking mutiny rather than harmony. Like the artist trying to draw the horse, homemakers need to take time out to get back in touch with their original image and evaluate as coolly as possible their attempts to fulfill that vision.

The person sketching has one big advantage over the homemaker: If she sets her materials down, she can count on finding them in the same condition when she returns. Our materials—people, place and time—aren't so cooperative. Instead of being inert, they are volatile. Children grow older; husbands change careers. The plumbing breaks down, and sons present us with homemade lamps that clash with our living rooms. And always, always, time passes much too quickly. Even homemakers who have a very clear idea of the homes they are working toward may find themselves panting, just trying to maintain what they have.

As a homemaker, I often feel like the little Dutch boy holding his finger in the dike, leaks sprouting all around him. There are so many broken glasses to sweep up and buttons to replace that sometimes it's hard for me to remember I ever had a vision, much less what it looked like. And yet we must hold to our dreams and do those things which breathe life into our hopes. We need to talk to other homemakers, to read books, to visit homes that inspire us. An artist without a vision is only a technician, and a home-maker without a dream is simply a housekeeper.

Our lives are a process of discarding some old visions, patching up others, and trying out new ones. We have the artist's flashes of inspiration when we finally think of a special activity to boost a child's sagging spirits or figure out a new system for organizing our storage space. For a while things go well, and then gradually we again get the sense that the sand is slipping out from under our feet. That sinking feeling is really an invitation to take another step forward. By our willingness to sharpen our vision and do the work necessary to make the dream a reality, the very special home that is meant for each of us takes its shape.

Memories

It is not enough for us simply to bring our own vision into reality, marvelous though it would be to really succeed in that. As parents we also want to pass our outlook on to our children. One of the most effective ways is through their childhood memories.

My current home is hugely influenced by the home I grew up in, a home which was filled with religious traditions. There are very few Advent or Lenten customs that my parents didn't try at least once. I have many happy memories of placing straws—representing my good deeds—into Baby Jesus' manger to soften it, or giggling helplessly at my father's attempts to sing on pitch during Lenten stations in the dining room. I made a conscious choice as an adult to be a Catholic, but the strong emotional ties binding me to Catholicism find their origin in the family traditions of my early childhood.

To some extent we are all motivated by a desire to recapture those wonderful moments of our childhood. Each Christmas we adults may be a little disappointed because the day is not as magical as we remember it. But when we string the lights and wrap the presents, the miracle is renewed in our children and grandchildren. The memories we create for our children when they are young will remain with them and will influence their actions when they grow older.

We are the custodians of our children's memories. Happy childhood memories are a marvelous legacy; they are like treasures stored in an attic to be taken out on a rainy day and pored over, perhaps even hugged. The quality of our children's early memories rests largely in our hands, and this is one painting which cannot be erased and done over. It is both a privilege and a responsibility to have such precious possessions entrusted to our care.

God's Vision for Us

Parents are not alone in their dreams for their families. There is one whose dream for us is brighter and more beautiful than we can imagine. St. Paul writes of "the things that no eye has seen and no ear has heard, things beyond the mind of man, all that God has prepared for those who love him" (1 Cor 2:9).

God is the only one who can create a physical reality using only his vision. While I have to slap on paint or shove heavy furniture across a room to make a change, he has only to think of a person and that person comes into existence. Out of his infinite knowledge and love, he has made each of us according to his own design.

Since God made us out of his perfect knowledge, it stands to reason that he has a clear idea of our possibilities. I once heard a lecture in which the Christian life was compared to cake mix. Quick-mix packages state clearly: "For best results, follow manufacturer's instructions."

Just as Pillsbury has a much better idea than I have of why two eggs will not make as successful a cake as three with their mix, so God knows exactly what we need to develop fully. He knows the hidden talents that we haven't yet discovered and the hidden flaws we haven't yet had the courage to disclose to anyone. Better than anyone else, he knows us, our circumstances, and how this family he so lovingly created can best grow to its full richness and maturity.

Fortunately for us, God is willing to let us have

some of this inside information. What we need to do is to learn to ask for the knowledge and to listen when it's shared. I have plenty of opinions about what's best for my home, but when I spend some quiet time in God's presence there is usually a subtle, or not so subtle, shift in my perspective. At times, the solution to a problem which has been nagging me for weeks will quietly, effortlessly, come to mind. Almost always, when I listen to God, my fundamental attitude changes. If I'm feeling discouraged and tense because things are difficult, part of the burden shifts to the shoulders of one who is stronger than I. Instead of feeling quite so self-important when things are going well, I am reminded that all I have—my family, my talents, my lovely old apple tree—are pure gift.

As Christian homemakers, our homes should be fundamentally different from those of our non-Christian neighbors. Some of those differences will be apparent to outsiders and others will not. One of those not-so-obvious differences is that we rely explicitly on the vision of God, the Master Artist, who provides us not only with the dream, but also with the means to realize it.

Art As Self-Expression

Jean-Baptiste Corot has said that a painting is a landscape seen through a particular temperament. If you set each member of your family to work painting the same clump of trees on a hillside with the sun sinking behind it, each person would produce a different picture. The children in our family, who are still young, would paint in broad strokes of orange and green. I would try to capture the sky's delicate shading from pink to red and the tranquil mood of the scene. On the other hand, my husband would pick out the silhouette of the trees against the sky, perhaps choosing black and white rather than color for his work. Other families would have comparable experiences with each member expressing a different perception of the same scene.

If so much variety exists within one family, then the differences between one family and another are even more dramatic. As Christian homemakers, we share the same fundamental goals. But each family has a particular flavor, a unique blend of ethnic background, opportunities, temperaments, and resources. The blend of these qualities can produce the special character of our homes.

To illustrate this, call to mind for a moment five homes that you have visited. Each house is distinct. Some are accented with natural woodwork and hand thrown pottery, others hold velvet La-Z-Boys and dark shelves lined with knickknacks. Some are immaculately kept, while others could best be described as lived-in. Some homes have a sense of being loved, while others seem sterile.

Go to a real-estate open house and you can discover a great deal about a family without ever seeing it. You can get a general idea of its income level and whether or not there are children. Kitchen shelves filled with cookbooks tell you that food is important, while religious art through the home indicates a family of faith.

We express ourselves in our homes by the colors we choose or the items we have available for recreation. People learn about us from the atmosphere they sense in our homes. The clearer sense we have of ourselves as persons, as family, and as God's creatures, the more completely we can integrate that idea into our vision of a home. We strive not to create *the* perfect home, but rather *our* perfect home—the home that best suits us and best expresses our own personalities.

The Artist and Her Materials

An effective artist must always understand and respect her materials. This is obvious on a purely practical level. One of the reasons I like to sew is that making my own clothes gives me an opportunity to express myself. However, if I decided to whip up a warm-up suit out of a nice piece of heavy wool I had on hand, the major aspect of my personality I would communicate would be a total disregard for reality.

I love to have fresh flowers in the house, but I have mastered only one technique of making bouquets. I get a short, squatty vase and stuff it as full of flowers as I can. My garden is filled with round and puffy zinnias, marigolds and asters which lend themselves well to my floral design. With those flowers I get pretty bouquets in my little pots; with gladioli, for instance, I'd have a mess.

Occupation?

A homemaker must suit her technique and her vision to her materials. It is not my job to dream up some concept of the ideal home and then try to lop off any stray parts of my family that don't fit into the mold. The results would be similar to my trying to shove those glads into my little teapot: a lot of mashed flowers and no bouquet.

I have a tendency to try to make my husband and children into mirror images of myself—minus my faults. I want them all to be voracious readers and avid gardeners. My husband doesn't enjoy reading, but is very gifted before an easel. If I try repeatedly to bully him into reading my favorite book in hopes of a scintillating discussion, what will scintillate instead will be his justified anger. But if I can appreciate his talent and encourage him in his painting, and he can listen patiently as I rattle on about my latest book, then together we produce a more balanced home than either of us could provide alone.

Some sculptors go so far as to say that when they work they do not create a new shape at all. Rather, they maintain that a form is hidden within a chosen block of wood, and their job is simply to discover and then uncover it. That is an attitude that is central to the homemaker's art.

Homemakers do not start from scratch. We choose our husbands, more or less, but our children are given to us. We choose our house or apartment, but that choice is limited by our financial resources and proximity to jobs and schools. The amount of time we have to spend with our families is cut into by many outside sources. It is the homemaker's job to take a penetrating look at her materials and match her vision to the possibilities found in those elements.

A woman on a tight budget will never be happy or successful if she spends her time yearning for hand-crafted furniture and catered dinner parties. The mother of teen-agers simply does not have the amount of family time that a mother of preschoolers has. The effective homemaker is gifted with the love and discernment to see what is truly possible in her home and the flexibility to adjust her vision as conditions change.

The fundamental attitude prompting an artist to work effectively with her materials is a profound appreciation of their worth. For example, I do not put the same care into sewing a gingham dress that I do into a jacket made of expensive wool. A woman who hates the house she's living in will not be able to recognize its good points and maximize them.

An effective artist must understand and respect her materials on a personal level as well. The people who have caused me to change most successfully have had confidence in me. They were not the people who tried to impress on me that my shortcomings were so miserable that even I should no longer be able to tolerate them. Rather, they had faith in my good intentions while they did not deny my failures. They gave me a sense of who I could become and the energy to try to attain that goal.

As homemakers we will be able to shape the elements of our homes most effectively if we act out of realistic but optimistic love for each of them.

Occupation?

Finally . . .

As homemaker/artists, we have high hopes and marvelous visions for the people and place entrusted to our care. And yet we must live with the knowledge that those dreams will never be fully realized in this lifetime.

We often think of heaven as the experience of seeing God in all his fullness. St. Paul describes it, "Now we are seeing a dim reflection in a mirror; but then we shall be seeing face to face" (1 Cor 13:12). God's face is not the only one that we shall behold for the first time. The vision we have now of our home and family is intermittent, glimpsed and then lost amid all our activity. On that day, after all our broken efforts, we will finally see one another—transformed into dazzling incarnations of that perfect vision from which we were all created.

The hazards of homemaking

It is inspiring to think of ourselves as artists, fashioning our homes into unique and memorable works of art. But the romance of being an artist is not without its risks. Poets and playwrights are known better for alcoholism and depression than for sunny dispositions, and homemaking, like the other arts, can be psychologically hazardous. The lack of recognition for our work, the loneliness, the sheer exhaustion of our job can wear away at our image of ourselves as bright, attractive women.

Our Investment

The most potent threat of all to our sense of security is our enormous emotional investment. Those of us who are home full time focus tremendous time, talent and energy on our home lives. By contrast, husbands with jobs and children at school spend a large portion of their days away from home. As a result, homemakers often feel as though we are paddling frantically upstream in a canoe filled with sightseers. It is usually the full-time homemaker who has the most practical concern for the quality of family life, the most determination to improve it—and the most work. This is not necessarily because we are the noblest member of the family, although this conclusion is tempting. Much of the difference has to do with time commitments.

No matter how much a husband may value his family, a breadwinner working 40 or more hours a week outside the home does not have the same emotional investment at home as a full-time homemaker. On a practical level the full-time homemaker will be more aware of, and vulnerable to, the situation at home. When I was teaching high school, I could completely forget about a morning argument with my husband as I went to school and began working with my students. Now that I am home full time, I can fume all day with no change of scene to distract me.

Further, there are careers and companies which demand not only time but a level of dedication which conflicts with home life. And some workers, whether by personality or upbringing or circumstances, use work as an escape from home and intimate relationships. But even if every homemaker married a perfect man who worked for a perfect company, and if she had perfect pregnancies which resulted in perfect children, there would still be a discrepancy between her emotional investment and that of her breadwinning husband. And this discrepancy places the homemaker at risk.

Our emotional investment at home differs from that of our children too. When children are young, home is the only world they know. The quality of their first years of life will shape the adult they become. But gradually children grow away from home, beginning the day they start preschool or kindergarten and culminating the day they move their belongings into a home of their own.

The risk for the full-time homemaker may be financial as well as emotional. Most of us know of at least one woman who has devoted five, 10 or 30 years to her family and then found herself divorced or widowed and struggling to support herself and the children she has with her. Two-thirds of all women entitled to support payments receive no money at all. It isn't surprising that families with a female head of household account for a disproportionately large percentage of the poor. There is a significant risk for a woman who steps out of a career to raise a family. I consider myself to be in a secure marriage, but in my heart I know that none of us is immune to divorce or widowhood, and it frightens me to see the price paid by those who lose the gamble.

Loneliness, Gift and Burden

Our children's inevitable growing-up process brings an element of loneliness to motherhood. When our first child was born, I was overwhelmed by the astonishing rush of love I felt for him. As I check our sleeping children at night, I am still awed that God has given them to us. But mingled with the joy I feel at having them with me is the disquieting sense that all this is temporary. When the baby takes his first steps, I share his exultant sense of victory while at the same time I am a little sad to know his energetic creeping is finished. I want to catch hold of these moments and preserve them somehow, but I know that with time even my memories will fade.

We remember our adolescent eagerness to be on our own, and we know that one day our children will be anxious to leave us. While it is proper that our children become independent, and it is a practical necessity for most husbands to be gone much of each day, the result for the homemaker can be a terrible loneliness. This loneliness is often most intense for homemakers whose husbands travel, or those struggling with a difficult or broken marriage.

Loneliness is certainly a common experience for women with very young children. No full-time homemaker is quite so full time as the mother of preschoolers. Women blessed with good neighbors or friends may enjoy these years as together they chat and push strollers around the block, but for other homemakers the preschool years can be terribly isolating. As fewer women choose to stay home, many homemakers find themselves the lone adult on the block after 9 a.m. And if they're not careful they can become the unpaid babysitter for all the neighborhood children after school.

Those who do not have access to a car can feel especially trapped. In our semi-rural area, I can easily go a week without seeing another adult besides my husband, and if I also happen to be short of sleep because I spent the night with a sick child, I can start to feel pretty sorry for myself.

We may feel that the one who should be most

ready to share our burdens—our husband—cannot understand us because his days are so different from ours. We love our children, and yet we are so often at odds with them. We can even become lonely for the self we once knew, the self who held her temper in check, who was well-groomed and even had enough energy left at the end of the day for a little romance.

If you relish homemaking and are blessed with a happy marriage and an abundance of friends, the next few pages may sound foreign to you. But they describe the feelings of women you know, women who need your gift of yourself.

The Effects of Loneliness

Any kind of pain, including loneliness, has the power to transform us. My great-aunt Mary, a single woman who devoted herself generously to her career as a nurse, spent her retirement living alone. Although her solitude was frequently broken by phone calls and visits, she was lonely, and as years went by she became negative and complaining. Illness caused her to spend the last year of her life in my parents' home, which is always bustling with activity. As Aunt Mary was slowly freed from her loneliness, her optimism and charm returned.

Homemakers engulfed by loneliness must also struggle against a tendency to draw inward. A few years into my homemaking career loneliness settled in and seemed destined to last forever. I was frightened to see the change in myself. I began to wonder whether I was lonely because of circumstance, or if there was something wrong with me. I was becoming insecure, pessimistic and angry.

Anger is a healthy response to pain, but anger must be handled effectively so that it does not become destructive. A friend confessed one day: "You know, I used to like myself. I saw myself as a happy person who liked other people. Now there are days when I wake up angry and the day just deteriorates from there." The temptation is to blame others for our situation and to become determined that our families recompense us for our losses. We become demanding complainers, and no one is more shocked by the change than we are.

If the pain of loneliness shakes us, it also challenges us. Friendship and loneliness are the light and dark sides of one reality; friendship is the presence of intimacy in our lives, while loneliness is our awareness of its absence. Just as the pain we feel when we brush against a hot stove warns us to pull away before we are seriously injured, so the pain of loneliness prompts us to knock down the walls barring us from one another. A person who loses the sense of sight becomes more aware of sounds and smells; so too, homemakers who have limited opportunity for friendships have a special appreciation for intimacy. As homemakers, our lives are dedicated to building relationships; loneliness is both the gift and the burden of our vocation.

Friendship

The obvious person for us to turn to in our

loneliness is our Lord. He is never too busy for us; on the contrary, it is we who become too busy for him.

Homemaking is a critical time for us to have a sense of contact with God. Those who find homemaking difficult need the security of knowing we are doing God's will, that he is with us and loves us even when the house is a mess and we are fat and pregnant. All of us need to know his presence so we can fulfill the essential task of introducing our children to friendship with him. And yet the early years of homemaking may be the most difficult time in our lives to maintain a good prayer life.

For several years before we had children, I consistently spent a half hour a day in prayer. I was able to maintain that pattern because I set aside the same time every day to pray. With my current irregular schedule as the mother of young children, I haven't been as successful in keeping up a consistent prayer life.

Many homemakers are told not to worry about the problem: "Your whole life is a prayer." Such advice is comparable to suggesting that we don't need to talk to our husbands and children since our cooking and cleaning is done out of love for them. Spouses who do not take the time to talk to each other become strangers, and our relationship with God is no different. Just as we need time alone with our husbands, so we also need time alone with the Lord. We strive for this not out of guilt, but because closeness to him is as nourishing and renewing as any intimacy we will encounter in our lives.

I am too easily distracted now to do the meditative kind of prayer I did before we had children, so I use more formal prayer, changing the format from time to time. For a few months I use scripture, then I try spiritual reading for a while, and sometimes I pray the rosary. I rely heavily on outside sources, a spiritual director and occasional classes on prayer. My prayer life is sporadic, and when it limps I get discouraged. I struggle to find a balance between being beset by guilt over my failures and becoming complacent and forgetting my efforts entirely.

Only hermits are meant to get through life relying solely on their relationship with God. For the rest of us, good friendships, preferably including close ties with other homemakers, are essential.

We not only need friendships—we have a right to them. In his encyclical *Laborem Exercens* Pope John Paul II speaks of workers' right of association. (This is one of the few pieces of literature I've seen which includes homemakers among "workers.") In referring to the right of association, the pope is speaking primarily of unions, and I am not proposing that we unionize. Unions, however, do not exist solely to negotiate wages and working conditions; an important function of unions and professional organizations is providing opportunities for workers in the same field to pool their knowledge and experience. Effective homemaking is an art requiring a vast array of skills, and without access to other homemakers we can spend much of our time reinventing the wheel.

Besides learning skills from other homemakers, we also need their emotional support. Those who have not been homemakers cannot really understand our lives. They do not know the joys that keep us where we are, nor the frustrations that make us consider leaving—for South America. And no one can laugh quite as hard, or quite as safely, about our trials as another homemaker.

So we need friends, we have a right to them. Homemakers, however, have some unique difficulties in forming these friendships.

The first problem is the popular image of the homemaker. This stereotype depicts homemakers as women who sit around all day, drinking coffee and discussing potty training. Anyone who has been through the ordeal of housebreaking a child knows that this is far from a trivial topic, but it does not dominate our conversations.

If anything is considered more typical of homemakers than kaffeeklatsching, it is yakking on the phone. The presupposition here is that women talk too much, and that phone conversations are a waste of time. As with most stereotypes, there may be some truth here. Some women do waste hours every day in gossip and small talk. Those homemakers who are blessed with an abundance of compatible neighbors or many telephone friendships need to bear this danger in mind. But we shouldn't allow the fear of confirming a stereotype prevent us from developing the friendships we need.

A second difficulty we encounter in forming friendships is the process itself. Non-homemakers generally find their friends through work or school. In that environment, they spend time with other people, engaged in some common activity. Certain people in the group will be drawn together, perhaps because they share an offbeat sense of humor or respect one another's integrity. Working side by side, they share time together and strike up conversations. Friendships arise naturally out of such situations.

In contrast, homemakers work alone. Scrubbing toilets does not require a team effort. We do not have the opportunity for spontaneous on-the-job friendships; instead, we meet people under artificial conditions. For instance, when we moved to our present house, a kind neighbor held a coffee party for the area. A dozen women came together, all eager to meet new friends but knowing absolutely nothing about one another. I got names and phone numbers of a few women and invited them to my house a few weeks later. There we looked at one another rather uncomfortably across the kitchen table and gamely made conversation. Some good friendships blossomed from those initial contacts, but the process involved more risk and awkwardness than casual contacts with co-workers.

Not only do homemakers need to be more deliberate about initiating friendships, mothers of preschoolers also find that the attention they can devote to friendships leaves something to be desired. Recently I had two invitations for lunch from mothers of young children, each living about 15 miles from my house. Twice I packed my children into the car, shouting myself hoarse as we tracked down security blankets and shoes that matched. On the road, the carsick baby added the usual measure of suspense to the journey. The other mothers, in their turn, spent the mornings cleaning the house and preparing one lunch for the children and another for the adults. We all put real effort into getting together, and I doubt that on either occasion we said three consecutive sentences on any topic. Instead we spent our time answering children's questions, pulling toddlers out of cupboards, and breaking up fights.

Not only do we expend extra effort to spend time with a friend, we also often pay a price afterward. One of the preschooler's major tasks seems to be building up immunity by catching every virus that drifts past. Last week, as I watched my four take turns losing their suppers to a stomach flu they picked up from our most recent guests, I asked myself if friendship was really necessary after all.

Mothers with older children tell me that our time doesn't become our own when the children enter school either. Mothers of school-age children are dictated to by carpools, orthodontist appointments and school activities. Later still, we are subject to frantic calls involving left-at-home textbooks, hockey equipment and college application forms. Even worse, we may get ready to meet a friend and find that one of the kids drove our car to school because he missed his ride. Interruptions may happen less often as the children get older, but the habit of expecting them can become part of our conversational pattern.

A third problem is that homemakers often find their job a difficult one to discuss. If I meet adults who are employed or in school, there are all sorts of questions I can ask about their job or course of study. On the other hand, people generally seem to be at a loss for something to ask me once they know I am a full-time homemaker. After asking my name and the size of my family, there seems to be nothing more to say.

Part of the difficulty here is the low status of homemakers. We live in a society which often judges people by their occupations. Occupations which require a great deal of training, or which command power or high financial rewards—medicine, law, finance—all confer status in our society. Homemakers have no formal training for their jobs, little power, and no salary! Thus in many circles homemaking is not a respected occupation, and most people—including most homemakers—assume that talk about our work will be boring. Certainly conquering the lime on the ceramic tile is not a topic with universal appeal. But that type of mundane detail is not limited to homemaking. It is part of every occupation. However, most people assume that there might be something interesting in other occupations. As homemakers we can't rely on the assumption that our job is interesting and worth talking about—quite the opposite.

If we fall into the trap of reporting rather than conversing, then we are more likely to stay at the level of small talk. "How are your children?" We review Matthew's soccer career. "And how is your husband?" We recount his current state of overwork or under-employment. While we yearn to share our hopes and struggles with someone else, it is much safer to stay at this level, to talk about the externals of our lives. We have to learn to take a chance and move from small talk to conversation.

It is important, though, to separate ourselves from our friendship-making skills. If we have difficulty talking to strangers, it does not mean that we are boring people; many fascinating people have not learned the art of beginning conversations gracefully. The conversation-starters we picked up at school or on the job don't necessarily help us as homemakers, and the solution is to develop some new skills.

Writer Judith Goldhaber correctly states that even the most mundane topics are fascinating when properly handled.[1] Instead of just giving facts, the skilled conversationalist moves on to feelings and ideas. For instance, instead of asking, "Where did you live before you moved here?" we can ask, "How did you feel about making your move?" Instead of giving the symptoms of our children's chicken pox, we can talk about the different ways various personalities respond to illness. Instead of asking which church a person attends, we can ask, "What is your parish like? How do you react to it?" Or, we can ask another homemaker how she feels about her decision to stay home.

An acquaintance's favorite conversation-starter is, "Tell me about. . . ." Rather than asking someone how many children she has, we can say, "Tell me about your family." This simple change invites a much more interesting response, one to which we can in turn respond creatively. All of these questions are

---

1. Judith Goldhaber, *Minneapolis Star and Tribune*, June 14, 1983.

safe and comfortable, but they help a conversation rise above the level of small talk.

Volunteer work in the parish or community can be a natural way to begin friendships. Volunteering puts us back in circumstances where we meet people in the course of an activity and conversation arises spontaneously out of our mutual concerns. I complained to an acquaintance that I didn't like going to parish functions because I was shy, and she advised me to pick up a coffeepot and start pouring. Serving is much less awkward than standing around and provides a perfect opportunity to introduce ourselves to new people.

Certainly our real concerns are not topics we just drop into casual conversations. Yet if we were able to talk more freely about loneliness, for example, perhaps we could escape it more readily. Sometimes we have to put ourselves at risk. I was rather uncomfortable broaching the subject of loneliness in my first homemaking class. The room was filled with competent women from my parish, and I was afraid that I would describe my feelings and then discover I was the only person there who was struggling. As I spoke, a normally cheery woman in the back of the room became visibly distressed. I was distracted from my notes, wondering if some family illness or other problem was troubling her. During the discussion period afterward I was astounded to learn that her tears had come because she felt as lonely as I. She would have been the last person in that room I would have suspected of being lonely. I have since discovered that many capable and sensitive homemakers are lonely, and that knowledge has given me the courage to speak out. I've found that loneliness is an emotion which all homemakers feel at times, and which some homemakers battle intensely. But there is a positive side. Handled creatively, loneliness heightens our awareness of our need for intimacy and spurs us to develop friendship-building skills which will benefit us at home and in the future.

Home, sweet home

The notion of *place*—the role places play in our lives, the process by which we shape the place we are in, our goals, and the elements with which we work—is basic material for the artist/homemaker. Indeed, the places of our lives are closely linked with our memories, our sense of security, and our sense of identity.

When we visit the places of our past, faces and emotions forgotten for years will suddenly come rushing back. When I drive past the grade school I attended, I can feel the innocence, excitement and uncertainty of those years. The faces of children flash through my imagination, children long grown up and traveling separate paths. When we visualize the place we spent our first year of marriage, and the adjustments, the youth, the freedom are made suddenly vivid. Places have an unparalleled power to evoke memories.

Places provide milestones for our lives. Our memories are divided into clumps, frequently according to the places we've lived. This happened when we lived in Tucson, or that happened when we were in the old house. As we review our lives, recalling the places we've lived, we discover a kaleidoscope of memories and emotions that are forever attached to those spots.

Most of us enjoy visiting our old haunts because the memories they hold are largely happy. But some of us would prefer not to visit certain places. If our teen-age years were awkward and lonely, we will not relish walking the halls of our high school during a reunion. A friend whose mother worked when she was growing up told of being left home alone with two older brothers who teased her unmercifully. She took refuge from them behind the locked door of the bathroom. Remembering that room brought back for her the loneliness and frustration of those hours.

Memories attached to places can be so strong that they cause us to behave as we did during our time spent there. When my mother visits me at my home, we relate as one adult to another. But when I return to her house, I have to fight my tendency to revert to childhood. I was dependent on my mother when I lived there, and when I return I unconsciously expect her to be in charge again.

Places also affect our sense of security. Human beings have an enormous need for love and security. Since we are not pure spirits, these needs are manifested and met in practical, physical ways. We show our love by putting an arm around someone and giving a hug. We demonstrate our appreciation with a smile, a thank you, or a gift of flowers. One manifestation of our deep need for security is the longing to have a place of our own where we can relax and be ourselves. As Paul Tournier writes: "Man is an incarnate being who needs a place and who needs to be attached to it and to be rooted in it."[1]

It is easy to see the importance of place if we consider the alternative: homelessness. Tournier writes of the neuroses he treated among World War II refugees, neuroses caused by the terrible anxiety people feel when they have been torn from their homelands. And Edward E. Hale's image of a man condemned to live out his days on a ship which no country will receive frightens and touches us.

The nation in which we live determines the language we speak, the way we dress, and even our sense of humor. Regions within a country produce their own unique flavors; a child growing up on a farm in Iowa is different from one in a Los Angeles barrio. Even in a small town, neighborhoods reflect income, nationality or religion.

When I was growing up, Catholics identified themselves according to parishes. If you asked people where they lived, the response would be "St. Luke's" or "Nativity" or "St. Leo's." Until I was 12 we lived in St. Therese's parish. People at St. Therese's dressed seriously, and we always wore white gloves to Sunday Mass. Then we moved two miles north to St. Mark's which was known more for the size of its families and the strength of its athletic teams than for its polish. Within months, my sisters and I had abandoned our white cotton gloves. We were more interested in leather softball mitts. A change in location had brought about a change in values.

---

1.   Paul Tournier, *A Place for You* (New York: Harper & Row, 1968), p. 52.

Just as a neighborhood or nation affects our identity, so the place we call home affects us. A spacious, formal, quiet house exerts a different influence than a small, noisy, casual house. A bright, sunny house cheers us and a dark, somber house depresses us because of a purely biological reaction our bodies have to varying light levels.

Scripture, which reveals human as well as divine nature, is filled with references to place. The opening chapters of Genesis describe God creating a place for the human race, a place perfectly designed for our happiness. The Garden of Eden was the perfect home. All needs were supplied and all creatures lived in harmony. Jews and Christians are not alone in their dream of a long-ago place which was lost by human failing; from the ancient Greeks to the American Indians, people have described such a spot. Paul Tournier says that we each have a "Paradise Lost complex," that the desire within us for a home is really a reflection of our longing for our ultimate home, heaven.

The saga of the Old Testament centers on the Jews' struggle to find and hold onto the Promised Land. When humanity lost its first home through sin, God promised a new home. In the New Testament, we are touched each Christmas by the poignant story of Mary and Joseph searching for a place in Bethlehem. As an adult, Jesus spoke of his lack of a home, "Foxes have holes and the birds of the air have nests, but the Son of Man has nowhere to lay his head" (Mt 8:20). These scriptural references reinforce our own experience of the importance of places.

When we understand the relation of place to our memories, our security and our sense of identity, the place we call home takes on new significance. Much of our time as *home*-makers is devoted to *place*-making.

The Place-making Process

We have all had the experience of coming into a place and immediately sensing it has been loved. For several years our family has spent our vacations in a lake cabin belonging to neighbors whose family has built it room by room over the past 70 years. Almost all the furniture there first saw service somewhere else, but the pieces have been carefully arranged and repainted. The wooden high chair is so charming that we don't mind having to tie the baby into it to keep him from slipping out of its oversize spaces. One bedroom is festooned with a collection of hats hung on nails on all four walls. The out-of-tune piano, the shelves of vintage novels, and the stacks of jigsaw puzzles and board games all have the marks of long usage. A collection of log books neatly stacked on a table contain entries from visitors over the last half-century, attesting to the happy times they have spent in the cabin.

Such a place touches all who enter it, because the people who have lived in it and loved it have left something of themselves behind. We have the same response to a handmade quilt or a hand-knit sweater. When we know someone has lavished hours of care on an article, we value it highly, even though a machine-made item may be technically more perfect. The old poem says:

> It takes a heap o' livin'
> in a house to make it home. . . .

And, as we have said in the previous chapter, homemakers have a large investment in turning their houses into homes. To succeed requires a certain attitude, a willingness to make a commitment, to put down roots.

When we were adolescents, the future held a tantalizing array of opportunities. We felt we could go anyplace, do anything, marry anyone. It is important to have such a time in our lives, but the time also comes to make a choice. We can look at our time, talents and energy as if they were money which we were going to invest. Some investors are so afraid of losing their money that they are incapable of risking any of it. On an emotional level this is echoed today by people who are afraid to commit themselves to a marriage, a career, or a cause in case something better turns up down the road. Other investors divide their money among several ventures, so they are assured of always having some money in case one or another investment fails. They are like people who marry and choose a career, but carefully parcel out their lives to avoid being truly vulnerable to either.

Still other investors sink everything into their hopes for one company, and we full-time homemakers share their recklessness. We take our talents, our time, and our energy and invest them in a very small patch of territory and a few people.

It is frightening to gather up our lives in our two hands and choose to invest so much of it in one place. There is wisdom in the old adage which cautions, *Don't put all your eggs in one basket.* Too many middle-aged and older women in America today are standing with empty baskets. None of us wants to be left in the position of having invested ourselves totally in our homes only to find ourselves years later with nothing. It takes enormous courage to look squarely at the risk involved and to choose it in spite of everything. But if we are willing to take the risk, we greatly increase our opportunities to bring our homes to life.

For our greatest risk is also the source of our greatest power. We have the power and time to transform a place simply because *we are there.* When we choose to spend ourselves in a place, that place cannot help taking on our spirit, for good or for ill, and it will transmit that spirit to others. We are like the grain of wheat in the gospel, burying ourselves, in a sense, to bring forth new life.

If this choice is hard to make, it is even more difficult to sustain. I tend to be like my father, who says he prefers to work at a project long enough so that he can tell what it would look like if he finished—and then move on to something else. A few years after we bought our present house I began to feel that familiar urge to move on. I had fallen in love with our house the moment I saw it, but before long I began to feel restless. I wished the house were a little larger, the setting a little more picturesque. I started watching the real estate ads, "just in case." And then I realized I had two alternatives. I could either move from house

59

to house, exploiting what others had put into them, or I could accept our house and invest myself in it. To choose to be an investor rather than a window shopper is not to say that I will never live in another house; rather it is a shift in attitude toward a willingness to put down roots, to invest time and self in *this* place.

The power we have to transform a place is shown in the following description of a Nazi prison cell:

> I had seen the home Betsie had made in Scheveningen. For unbelievably, against all logic, the cell was charming. . . . The straw pallets were rolled instead of piled in a heap, standing like little pillars along the walls, each with a lady's hat atop it. A headscarf had somehow been hung along the wall. The contents of several food packages were arranged on a small shelf; I could just hear Betsie saying, "The red biscuit tin here in the center!" Even the coats hanging on their hooks were part of the welcome of that room, each sleeve draped over the shoulder of the coat next to it like a row of dancing children. It had been a glimpse only, two seconds at the most, but I walked through the corridors of Scheveningen with Betsie's singing spirit at my side.[2]

Once we become aware of our power as homemakers to transform a place by our presence and commitment, then we can begin to explore the process of shaping our environment. There is a dynamic relationship between our families and the

2. Corrie ten Boom, *The Hiding Place* (New York: Bantam Books, 1974), p. 163.

spaces we inhabit; we alter our places to suit our purposes, and they in turn shape us according to their character.

The Montessori method of education is based on the concept of providing an environment prepared to promote maximum learning. In *The Secret of Childhood*, Maria Montessori compares the child in school to the fetus in the womb. A pregnant mother does nothing to direct her baby's growth; she provides the environment and the resources, and the fetus matures according to the guiding principle within it. No one tells a fetus to grow 10 fingers and two ears—some mysterious force within commands that the necessary human equipment appear at the proper time. Montessori holds that the same inner principle guiding our physical development is also at work in our intellectual, emotional and spiritual development. The homemaker's job is to provide the resources and environment so that our family's intellects, emotions and spirits can unfold and expand according to God's design.

Psychologist Burton White in his classic work, *The First Three Years of Life*, confirms this notion. His studies indicate that most people do a good job of parenting during their children's first year, but that when children reach a year of age many parents make the mistake of allowing them to become overly attached to their mothers at the expense of independent learning and exploration. He agrees with Maria Montessori that a major responsibility for those who care for children is shaping the proper environment.

Adults also require a good environment. As homemakers, it is our job to provide environments that will call forth the profoundly human qualities of our families.

Setting Priorities

Homes cannot develop a shape unless there is some clarity and agreement about the values held by their homemakers. We direct our time and our energy toward those things we value. If our values are not clear to us, or if there is a basic conflict in values between spouses, then inconsistent choices are made and the home is shapeless.

Setting priorities is best done as a communal effort. A study on school furniture[3] revealed that students, maintenance people and administrators could all offer valuable information about school furniture to manufacturers. Administrators want good appearance and sturdy construction, maintenance people look for ease in cleaning and upkeep, and students want comfort. But the manufacturers of school furniture never thought to ask the users for advice on design.

A comparable situation often exists in our homes. Most often it is the homemaker who arranges furniture and chooses a color scheme for the home. Flip through the bedroom ensembles in any mail-order catalog and ask yourself what proportion of those outfits would be purchased by a man. Like the school furniture manufacturers, we are trying to meet people's needs, but we don't always think to ask for

---

3.   L. K. Pinnell, "Functionality of Elementary School Desks," Bureau of Laboratory Schools Publication No. 5.

information from the people who can best give it to us. We're often disappointed because our families don't notice when we make a change in the house. If we invite them to participate in the decision-making, we may generate not only some interest but some help as well. If the family can set up goals and explore place-making possibilities together, then our homemaking efforts will be much more effective.

An advantage to including the whole household in the decision-making process is that our environments will then be more responsive to the changing needs of our families. Our houses change, and more important, the people within them change. We need to use our homes differently when we are surrounded by preschoolers (when a major concern is getting them out from underfoot) than when we are living with teen-agers (when the concern may be prying them out from behind closed bedroom doors or away from the telephone).

Christian homemakers have many goals to consider in establishing the priorities for our places. One is our relationship with God.

Years ago, it was easy for people to know when they had entered a Catholic home. There were crucifixes on several walls, and often a picture of the Sacred Heart or St. Therese of Lisieux tucked somewhere. The back yard might hold a statue of St. Francis, birds alighting on his head and hands, or perhaps a flowered shrine to the Blessed Virgin made from a carefully propped-up bathtub. With the renewal of the 1960s came a wave of criticism against the kind of religious art found in most homes. The unfortunate result is that very few of my contemporaries display *any* religious art.

With all their flaws, the pictures and statues we grew up with did serve as a constant reminder of God's presence among us. A family's choice to hang a crucifix or light a vigil candle during May was a witness to visitors and growing children of the Lord's importance in that home.

The one type of religious art which most people do buy is a Nativity set. Most families display a creche at Christmas, and it is interesting to note that many of the figures look exactly like those in sets sold 100 years ago. The crib set is a central part of our celebration of Christmas, balancing the Christmas tree and all the gifts. Standing as a silent reminder of the reason behind the festivities, the creche is an example of the power of religious art in the home.

Besides searching for Christian art for our homes, we can foster our family's relationship with God by setting aside a special place for prayer. Some charismatic households today set aside a whole room to be used only for prayer, and a remarkable peace comes to dwell in those places. Most of us cannot afford a whole room, but some kind of prayer location can be a wonderful invitation to pray.

Our prayer spot is in the children's playroom. I cover the top of a dresser with a piece of fabric colored for the liturgical season: purple for Lent and Advent, red for Pentecost, green for Ordinary Time, white for Christmas and Easter. On top of the fabric we arrange a live plant, a children's Bible on a stand, and a thick candle the color of the fabric.

When we prayed in the children's bedrooms at night, I was dismayed to find that my 6-year-old son was already beginning to groan when I announced prayer time. After we began using our special spot, the children got caught up in the special atmosphere. Gathering around the lighted candle to pray and sing has become a highlight of the day.

There are still days when we don't pray, and even then the prayer spot serves its purpose. If I look at that dresser on a day when I am neglecting prayer, it reminds me of the special times we have had together and how important it is to make the effort to pray with the children. When we arrange our homes with a portion especially dedicated to God, then that place silently calls us to become the Christ-centered people we hope to be.

Another goal we instinctively work toward is creating a place of beauty. We are uplifted by beauty, and a beautiful home is inviting to visitors and family members alike.

There are many opinions concerning what constitutes a beautiful house. We are delighted by some people's taste and appalled at others'. As homemakers, we do not need to become experts on the theory of interior decorating; rather, we need to choose the beautiful whenever possible.

Such a goal does not have to be in conflict with a limited budget or a commitment to simple living. One of the most charming homes I have ever visited was sparely furnished, and we ate supper on benches in the kitchen. The living room was illuminated by a chandelier of clay pots, suspended upside down from the ceiling with lightbulbs tucked inside. The very modest furnishings had been arranged tastefully and with care, and the effect was delightful.

Some people are more talented than others in home decorating, and it can take years to get a home pulled together. But our concern for the practical should not let us lose sight of the beautiful. Something as simple and inexpensive as growing flowers for the kitchen table can provide the dash of beauty we need on a gray day.

The following exercise can help us define some of our goals. Imagine being in solitary confinement. The only equipment in your cell is a set of barbells. No matter how much you might hate body building, after a few days of utter boredom you would probably begin hefting some weights. After an extended stay in that cell, you might develop an impressive set of muscles, although the rest of you would be suffering from lack of stimulation.

Suppose, on the other hand, you found only a clock, some tools, and a manual on watch repair in your cell. Whether or not you had any previous interest in the intricacies of clockwork, after a few weeks with nothing else to do you would probably develop a working knowledge of watchmaking.

Especially when they are young, our children are in a similar situation. They are in our homes with very little access to the outside world, and all that's available for their development are the materials we provide. If we have plenty of paper, paints and crayons, their artistic talents will blossom. If we have musical instruments and a stereo, they can explore music. If there are bats and balls, they can exercise their bodies. Our homes foster various aspects of personality by the equipment they hold.

Imagine once again that you are in that isolation cell. What would be the 10 things you would most want to have with you? Would you hope for a cozy, comfortable chair? a Bible? a piano? a window box with flowers? The answers reflect your values.

Now, ask the other people in your home the same question: *If you were in isolation, what 10 things would you want to have with you?* Then take a critical look at your house. Does it encourage the activities you value? Does it fill the needs of the members of your family?

As we see the unique values of our families and set our priorities accordingly, we can begin to creatively and effectively shape a place which encourages those goals.

"The Genius of the Place"

A moment's reflection reveals that places do indeed have personalities of their own. Imagine stepping into a church on a warm summer day. The bright sunlight and bustle outside is left behind, replaced by the cool stillness of the church. Whether a place of worship has been used by Christians, Jews or Moslems, it has a presence which is strikingly different from the parking lot outside.

Some places which are untouched by human hands have magnificent personalities all their own. The Grand Canyon, the Maine seacoast, and the deserts of the Southwest all have grandeur and sweep that fascinate and humble us. Other places, like churches and hospitals, take on personalities because of human influence. A passenger in a train can easily discern the transition from France to Germany—the cluttered, weathered farm homes of France give way in a matter of miles to the meticulously maintained German houses. The countryside has taken on the character of the culture which inhabits it.

The personality of a place reflects the interaction between the innate character of the spot and the people who use it. The adobe mission churches of California resulted from Spanish culture blending with Southwestern climate and native materials. The totally different fishing villages on the Eastern seaboard are, by contrast, the result of English people settling in forested lands splashed by sea spray.

Alexander Pope wrote, "Consult the genius of the place in all." When we choose a place to live, we should give careful consideration to its personality. Our best efforts at place-making will come from developing the existing character of a place rather than struggling to turn it into something else. I can choose to fill my boxy Midwestern farmhouse with French provincial furniture, but I will be much more successful in creating an integrated place if I choose a style more in harmony with the house.

When we have chosen our place and acknowledged its spirit, then we can set about making it into a home. As we do so, our place takes on a sacred quality.

Modern people, perhaps Americans in particular, do not have the same awareness of sacred space as did people in earlier centuries. Perhaps we would agree that Rome and Lourdes, Fatima and Guadalupe are somehow special, but few of us think much about them. Churches built today, often designed as multi-use facilities rather than spaces set aside strictly for worship, often do not have the same sense of sacredness found in more traditional churches.

To say that we have lost some awareness of sacred places is not to say that we have lost a need for sacred space. Just as Bethlehem is sacred to us because God manifested himself dramatically there, so our homes take on a quality of sacredness because so much of our growth in him takes place there. The old customs of a groom carrying his bride over the threshold, of men doffing their hats as they entered a home, or the church's tradition of blessing a new home indicate our awareness that home space is different from other space and is worthy of special respect. Part of our dignity and power as homemakers rests on the long-recognized sacredness of the home.

When we consult the genius of our place, as Alexander Pope advises, we do not look only at the building in which we live. Childhood memories do not include simply a house, but also involve the route we walked to school, the roads or streets we bicycled, the trees and streams or neighborhood playgrounds. Yards and neighborhoods are integral parts of our home spot, and people looking for new homes instinctively consider them in making a choice. The ethnic mix of our neighbors, as well as their educational and income levels, have a strong impact on us and our families.

Everything in Its Place

Chipmunks' underground burrows are divided into distinct rooms devoted to various purposes. Some rooms are used for storing food, others for sleeping, and still others for social activity. People also prefer to divide their space; the thought of a family eating, sleeping, cooking and socializing in the same room is not inviting. The more clearly we can adapt spaces to certain activities, the more effectively those places can promote their purposes.

For example, people learn more effectively in a place set aside especially for studying. The fact that we have spent time studying in a place disposes us to a studying frame of mind when we again enter that spot. Similarly, clinics for insomniacs advise their clients to use beds only for sleeping, never for reading, watching TV or eating. When a patient is having trouble sleeping, he is told to get out of bed rather than remain in it, staring at the ceiling. Eventually the person associates bed only with sleeping and will feel sleepy upon climbing into bed.

Our house is too small to set aside whole rooms for certain activities, but I still find it valuable to establish distinct areas in the rooms. If I didn't have a desk for my writing and sewing materials, for instance, our children's sleeves would not reach past their elbows and this book would never have been written. Our prayer spot invites us to spend time with the Lord, and the children's game table encourages their craft projects and card games. We even have a "crabbing" spot where someone who has lost an argument but still needs to vent some feelings can complain without annoying the rest of us.

We can learn a great deal about the power structure within our families by observing our use of space. Robert Sommer writes: "There is a close connection between space and status. Higher-ups have more and better space, as well as greater freedom to move about. This becomes institutionalized in the design and layout of buildings."[4]

In the past, the parents, and in particular the father, dominated the home. For instance, the father generally sat at the head of the table to represent his position as head of the house. Even in biblical times, the host was seated at the head of the table with honored guests at his side. A group of people seated at a rectangular table and asked to elect a chairman will generally elect the person seated at the head of the table. The father's position at the head of the table not only expressed his dominance, it also reinforced it.

We laugh at Archie Bunker's jealously guarded chair because so many of us grew up in homes where Father had "his" chair. Father's chair was generally the largest and most impressive in the house, and even fathers who allowed others sitting privileges expected the seat to be vacated when they were ready to use it.

---

4. Robert Sommer, *Personal Space: The Behavioral Basis of Design* (Englewood Cliffs, NJ: Prentice-Hall, 1969).

If fathers tend to express their family position by their seating arrangements, homemakers set their boundaries in other ways. One technique is house cleaning. If I scrub the kitchen floor and the children track mud on it, I feel that somehow they have trespassed on "my" property. A homemaker who keeps a spotless house, insisting that those who use a room remove any signs of their presence before leaving, may be saying, "This is my territory. You use it only by permission."

When I started reflecting on our family's use of space, I realized that I had taken over more space than I deserved. Cleaning would be the very last tactic I would use, but storing junk is a good substitute. I have boxes loaded with craft supplies, old letters, scrapbooks and clothing stashed under every bed and in every closet in the house. Whenever I come across a stray hammer or screwdriver of my husband's, I put it in the garage or balance it on his already overloaded dresser, but my knitting and sewing baskets are scattered through every room of the house.

Past hierarchical family patterns have tended to give way to a more democratic system. Where Victorian children were not allowed in the parlor and were expected to be seen and not heard, modern American children generally have the run of the house. This is due, in part, to smaller families living in larger houses. As animals become crowded, their hierarchical system gets more rigid and well-defined, and the same generally holds true for people. If I were raising our four children in our house 80 years ago, when it consisted of one small room, I could get mighty dictatorial, too.

In some homes, it is the children who control the space. A French neighbor, discussing a mother who was overwhelmed by a pair of twin toddlers said, "Her house is like all American houses—no doors!" While I prefer the American style of childrearing which allows children the freedom of the house, I would agree with my French friend that children should not dominate the territory.

By examining the way in which space in our homes is divided, we can learn about our family's internal structure. If we decide to make some changes in the family's interaction, we can shape our space in order to facilitate that change.

The size of our homes and the way in which we use our space can foster intimacy, privacy, or a happy blend of both. Americans are known for placing an emphasis on freedom and independence, and we require an extraordinary amount of space in order to feel comfortable. People in most other cultures are accustomed to far less. A Latin-American official, for instance, showing off an 18' x 20' room which housed 17 clerks at individual desks remarked, "See, we have nice spacious offices. Plenty of space for everyone."[5]

Perhaps our cultural need for independence takes a toll on family relationships. As we strive to raise children who are capable of close, lasting relationships, we would do well to question whether our houses foster intimacy. Robert Sommer was called in

5. Sommer, op. cit., p. 68.

as a consultant by the staff of a nursing home who were concerned about the low level of interaction among the residents. The home had just been remodeled, and all the new furniture had been neatly arranged along the long walls of the lobby. Residents sat in the chairs, side by side, staring straight ahead and rarely speaking to one another. Sommer rearranged the chairs, grouping them around small tables, and put fresh flowers and new magazines around the room. Solely as a result of these changes, residents began to move to the center of the room, sitting together in small groups, reading and talking together.

Homemakers can also arrange our homes to promote conversation. A rambling house with private bedrooms for each person protects privacy, but it does not necessarily encourage close relationships. In a large house it is important to provide communal space which draws people together. A large, comfortable kitchen is ideal, as is a well-used family room. When I was growing up, my mother constantly arranged conversation spots in our large house; my father complained that we didn't need wall-to-wall carpeting because we had wall-to-wall tables. As children we used to chuckle at her efforts, but now as a homemaker I understand her goals and admire her insight.

While those in large homes may find their houses afford too much privacy, those of us who are cramming large families into small houses have the opposite concern of protecting privacy. Studies with both animals and people indicate that the greater the degree of crowding, the more importance individuals attach to having a small place or thing which they can call their own. In particular, it is important for the relatively powerless people in the group to have some things which are truly their own.

Very young children do not seem to have the same need for privacy found in adults. Infants sleep comfortably in a crib, a dresser drawer, or draped across someone's shoulder. My toddlers can carry on a conversation in a nose-to-nose position that makes my eyes cross. But as children grow older, they develop a need for personal space which peaks during adolescence. Protecting their privacy by providing them with the breathing space they need can help promote harmony in the home.

Different families will prefer varying degrees of intimacy and privacy, authority and equality. The amount of space we have to work with, our division of space for individual and common use, and the amount of control exerted by various family members all contribute to the unique character of our homes.

Our attachment to place extends to an attachment to objects in that place. Linus' ever-present security blanket is duplicated in many homes, and many a homemaker has been embarrassed by the tattered shreds her child insists on dragging around.

Residents of nursing homes cling to the knick-knacks and pictures they bring with them, fragile links to their past. When we move into a new house or apartment, we can't rest until the furniture is in place and the cupboards are filled; only then does the place seem like home. A satisfying home is one which contains objects that comfort us, give us joy, and anchor us to our place.

Color consultants are cropping up all over the country, developing a thriving business advising people how best to use color to enhance their personal appearance. Where beauty consultants' advice is based on hair and eye color and skin tone, the homemaker's concern is with the effect that color has on the atmosphere of her home. Restaurants and hospitals have conducted costly studies to determine the effects of color on people's moods, and homemakers who choose a color scheme without taking this factor into account will probably regret their choices.

Each of us has distinct color preferences; we generally choose those colors which look best on us. Taking the lovely color of our favorite blouse and transferring it to a wall can have dreadful results. As homemakers our main concern is whether a color is warm or cool, restful or energizing. Whatever our favorite colors, they can generally take on the emotional characteristics we would like by altering the shade or hue: there are warm grays and cool grays, vibrant yellows and soft yellows. My own color consultant, my architect father, has saved me from some disastrous choices. Recently I showed him some paint chips I had carefully matched to my wallpaper, and he corrected my choices by finding warmer shades of the colors I had chosen. When my project was finished, I thought it was perfectly charming, but I realized I would have hated the results if I had stuck with my original colors.

A good book on color theory can be helpful, but most people require training and experience to be able to distinguish a cool (blue) red from a warm (orange) red. When we seek out a knowledgeable friend or a home decorator for advice, we don't have to turn over the selection of colors to them. Rather, we need to decide what kind of mood we want to establish in our homes and then ask for help in finding a shade of our chosen colors which will create that atmosphere.

A final element to consider is the noise level in our homes. Each of us has an individual tolerance for noise which is partly innate and partly the result of our upbringing. I like quiet; my husband, on the other hand, becomes uncomfortable without some sound in the background. While we have limited control over the noise of conversation and everyday living, we can alter the amount of mechanical noise from stereo, radio and television.

As with all other elements we have discussed, there is no ideal noise level. Rather, noise is an element which, unmanaged, can have a negative effect on home life, but which has the potential of becoming an asset.

Music can be a potent force in establishing the mood of a home. We associate candlelight, a quiet atmosphere, and soft music with romance. Classical music in the background is appropriate for a formal dinner, but at picnics our selections may be loud and boisterous.

Most libraries have a good supply of well-chosen children's records which can give a lift to both children and parents. Good religious music can help me lift my heart to God. A favorite record can give me the energy to tackle my housework on a morning when I am having trouble shifting out of first gear. My mother used to rush to the stereo and play lullabies when things became frantic at our house; she was convinced that the melodies had a soothing effect on us. It's a theory I keep intending to test on my own children.

The Christian Homemaker's Perspective

The Christian homemaker's unique challenge is to invest herself in her home. Yet, because we spend so much of our time at home working with things, we must be aware that the homemaking vocation carries with it a special risk of materialism.

Before I was married, I prided myself on my freedom from material things. I moved often and could pack all my belongings in a Volkswagen. Then my husband and I moved to our first apartment, our lovely wedding gifts surrounded by the odds and ends of furniture we brought with us. Now that I was married, I began to want silverware that matched and towels that coordinated with the bathroom. As our children arrived, I wanted them to have nice things. For the first time in my life I found myself struggling against a too-great attachment to things.

As we said earlier, beauty is a valid goal of the homemaker. But it must be balanced against the Christian call to simple living. Pope John XXIII told us that Christians are called to live simply in accordance with their station in life. An accountant needs to spend money on clothing which a pipe fitter does not, but both are called to generosity. God calls some people to voluntary poverty and blesses others with comparative wealth. Each of us needs to listen to his call to us, respecting that each person's vocation is distinct.

Our children will learn much about their relationships with things from our example. If we are careless and wasteful of our possessions, they are likely to duplicate our behavior. If we are careful stewards, respecting our possessions as gifts which have been temporarily bestowed on us, they will learn to do the same.

A couple I know live in a colonial house in Massachusetts furnished with exquisite antiques. Their precious things are not simply left on display, but are used every day in cooking and dining. One day when I was visiting, a friend dropped and broke a lovely plate as we washed the dishes. Her dismay was met by prompt and heartfelt reassurance from the owners that things are meant to be treasured and carefully handled while we have them, but not mourned when they are lost. This attitude of appreciating and being grateful for things, yet remaining free of them, should be expanded to our relationship with our homes as a whole. Paul Tournier compares life to a trapeze act. The trapeze artist must have a firm grip on the first swing before swinging forward and catching hold of the next. But a trapeze act in which the artist got a firm grip on that first bar and never let go would be boring indeed. Homemaking is the same. We work with the materials of our vocation as we meet changing needs; we don't try to acquire things and hold tight to them. Unless we learn when to let go, we will not progress.

The fundamental purpose behind Christian homemaking is to provide our families with the security they need to make the leap into faith. Those who have never had the security of a healthy home are like the Vietnamese orphan adopted by an acquaintance of mine. Every night of her first week in her new home, she went to bed clutching a loaf of bread. She was so fearful of being without food that she was unable to relax or concentrate on anything else. People who have never been emotionally "at home" are in a similar position; they are so worried about their psychic survival, about being accepted, that they are incapable of risking generosity with God or other people.

To understand the full reality of Christian homemaking, we must not see ourselves as building a nest which is at the center of the universe, but as making a beautiful, precious resting spot on a long journey. No matter how rich and full a home we may be privileged to build, or how meager and broken it may be because of financial or emotional poverty, this home that we passionately love is only temporary. We are pilgrims—richly endowed, but pilgrims nonetheless. We are hard at work creating the very best homes we can, so that when the time comes, we may travel without fear to our true home.

The value and dignity of work

There's one sure way to distinguish between the heavenly home that awaits us and the one we live in today: The earthly home is the one with dust on the windowsills. It's valuable for us to understand that places play a significant role in our lives because keeping them up takes such a significant chunk out of our lives. I remember calling my sister and brother-in-law about a week after they had settled into their first house. I expected to hear glowing accounts of how wonderful it was to have a place of their own; instead, their first comment was, "My gosh, it's so much *work*!" By itself, a house is demanding, and if a few children are littering the place, the amount of work can be staggering. Further, many of the routine tasks involved in keeping a house going—cleaning, cooking, laundry—can be downright boring.

Vacuuming floors is not a fascinating job—especially if you're vacuuming the same floor for the 500th time. My 2-year-old thinks it's fascinating, but that's because he isn't allowed to do it yet. Once you've learned how to sort laundry, you'll probably sort it the same way for the rest of your life. And probably every day of your life—because housework is also repetitive. Everything we clean gets dirty again, sometimes before we even finish cleaning it. As one despairing homemaker protested, "It's terrible not to be able to accomplish anything that can't be destroyed in 10 minutes by a 2-year-old with a graham cracker!"

In fact, our efforts are often invisible to others, and sometimes to ourselves. Bad housekeeping is a lot more noticeable than good—if you ever feel the need to be complimented for sweeping the floor, just let the dirt collect on it for a few weeks first. People will notice cobwebs clinging to the ceilings, but if we dutifully wipe them out as soon as they threaten, no one will ever realize the effort involved.

The results of work disappear much too quickly. A meal that takes hours to prepare requires just minutes to consume. If I fold all the clothes in my children's drawers, they get disarranged the first time they are in a hurry to find a favorite shirt. Recently I decided to really clean an upstairs bedroom. I took my youngest child with me and spent a couple of hours scrubbing walls, cleaning windows, taking down curtains and vacuuming corners. When I finished, I felt very pleased with my progress; I dumped my bucket, tucked my son under my arm, and headed downstairs. What I had forgotten was that my other three children were loose in the house and the downstairs, which had been presentable when I left it, was now a shambles. I felt, as I so often do, as though I had taken one step forward and three backward.

Housework consumes our time and energy. We

begin the day with plenty of ambition and plans for interesting things we can do for ourselves and our children—as soon as we get the place straightened. Too often the end of the day comes and the house still doesn't look terrific, but the effort to get it clean has taken all the time and energy we had intended to use elsewhere.

Nor does our culture place a high value on physical labor. A white-collar job tends to be more prestigious than a blue-collar job, even though the blue-collar job may require a greater degree of skill, ingenuity and discipline. Housework is physical labor, and although I know washing dishes is necessary, it's hard for me to feel that it's very significant.

We sell ourselves short if we see our work as simply a necessary evil which must be dispatched as quickly as possible. In order to cope with the demands and frustrations of our occupation, we need to discover the dignity and importance of our work itself.

Is the Worker Deserving of Her Wages?

Some people maintain that homemaking will never achieve any dignity or status until homemakers are paid for their work. Certainly salary and status are closely related, and the homemaker's lack of salary makes some people see the job itself as unimportant.

However, there are more important indicators of value than money. Because we grew up in a wage society, we tend to assume that wages have always been a measure of valuable work. A century ago, however, that was not the case. The majority of Americans were farmers, many of them working at a subsistence level. Money was scarce, and husbands and wives strove together to produce the goods needed for the family; any excess goods were sold or bartered. Both partners worked hard, and it was obvious that the skills of both were necessary for survival. Their work was valued.

But with the coming of industrialization and urbanization, workers left home to find jobs, and in return earned salaries. Eventually a dwindling number of farmers, a few small businessmen, and homemakers were the only workers found at home.

Whatever her feelings about being paid for her work, the homemaker can discover her worth in other ways: by a look at the value of the work for other people, by its role in personal development, and by drawing on the church's theology of work.

The Value of Our Work For Others

Our work is important to our families because it produces and maintains the vital place which we discussed in the last chapter. The beauty and charm of an inviting home cannot exist without a lot of elbow grease. By our work we produce a place that comforts people and expresses our family's unique character. But while our basic goal is to shape our place into a vital home, most of our actual work is devoted to keeping the place from falling apart. Homes have a tendency to sink into disorder, and the goal of good housekeeping is good order.

I am not a naturally good housekeeper. As a matter of fact, I am a naturally terrible housekeeper. It's not so much that I dislike cleaning, but there are so many other things I prefer to do. Those of us who share a devil-may-care approach to housekeeping have a special need to take a hard look at the value of order in family life.

When I first became a homemaker, I took comfort in the poster I saw on someone's wall: *My home is clean enough to be healthy and messy enough to be happy.* If mess was an indication of happiness, then I had the happiest home in town. But, contrary to that principle, I gradually began to notice that the messier the house, the *less* happy I became. Some days my disposition deteriorated, and finally I would realize that my crankiness stemmed from the fact that I could not walk six feet in any one direction without tripping over something. I was most likely to let the house fall into disarray when I was feeling tired and discouraged. A messy house is often a cause for—and an expression of—depression.

Over the years I've come to believe that even terrible housekeepers like me have an innate desire for order. Pulitzer Prize-winning author Rene Dubos holds that many of our emotions reflect evolved instincts which were once necessary for survival. For instance, there was a time when people depended on lakes and rivers for their water. Now, although we get our water from a faucet and rarely give a thought to its source, many people still dream of a house on a lake or ocean. We feel secure, anchored, and at peace on the shores of a great lake, and we are fascinated by a running brook. Again, we no longer need fire to cook our food or warm our bodies; our furnaces invisibly heat our houses, and many of us cook on metal coils heated by electricity. But a cozy fireplace still comforts us, and we feel a special closeness with other people when we silently watch the flickering flames.

Most mammals that live in enclosed places have an instinct for cleanliness, but there is often a special nesting instinct in females. One of the things I've enjoyed most about raising rabbits is watching the marvelous preparations the mother makes for her litter. A few days before the bunnies are to be born, we place a box filled with straw in the mother's cage. She then gets busy arranging the straw, shaping a round pocket with tight sides that prevent the bunnies from burrowing through into the cold. She then pulls tufts of fur from her belly and lines the nest, mounding more fluffy fur over the babies after they're born. The tiny, hairless bunnies, weighing less than an ounce apiece, survive sub-zero weather in the cozy nest built by their mother.

Nesting behavior in our rabbits is prompted by the hormonal shifts of pregnancy and lactation. While we humans share some instincts with animals, we also differ radically from them because we are not ruled by instinct. Our decisions are conscious. We can observe that, for whatever reason, most people feel happier and are more pleasant to one another when they are in an orderly environment. We can choose to establish orderly homes because we see that external order contributes to internal harmony. And we can decide how best to implement that orderliness for the unique individuals who make up our families.

I spent a lot of time pondering the value of order in an effort to motivate myself to keep our house clean. The first time I taught a class on Christian homemaking, I took great pains to explain all my hard-won insights. I could tell by the way women were nodding their heads that most of them already knew the value of a clean house. The struggle for many is freeing themselves from a compulsion to have a clean house at all times and at any cost. One woman described her grandmother who had scrubbed her kitchen floor every day of her life. This meticulous lady's comment to her granddaughter was, "It's too late for me, but don't you ever become a slave to your house!"

A clean house is certainly important, but never as an end in itself. It is a real tragedy if children grow up feeling that furniture is more important than they are. Homemakers, too, need to know that they are more important than the house; sometimes, time for prayer comes before vacuuming. Once in a while, even time for tennis comes before vacuuming.

Every homemaker needs to achieve her own balance of order and comfort; this is one of the many areas where God has a vision for us based on our unique talents. I have a friend whose home is a delight to enter. Every piece of furniture, every towel and knickknack, has been carefully chosen and cared for, and the total effect is hospitable and lovely. That house is her gift to everyone who enters it. My house will never look like that, even when my children are no longer dumping flour on the steps or shredding paper in the living room. She and I have distinct gifts, and I am very glad to be able to enjoy hers.

In praise of homemaking

"Home Is the First School of Work"[1]

Good workers who wholeheartedly tackle a job and stick with it until it's finished are hard to come by. Home is the ideal place for children to learn a positive attitude toward work, but too often we neglect to teach our children. Those of us afflicted with a slap-dash approach to housework unconsciously pass our work habits on to our children. And highly efficient homemakers sometimes prefer to do all the housework themselves rather than going to the trouble of teaching children to do a job.

A good worker has the ability to overcome the inertia that prevents her from getting started on a job in the first place. Other than putting three meals on the table every day and dressing ourselves before we're seen by another adult, there are very few things a homemaker *must* complete at home in any one day. This freedom can be a danger. Without self-discipline, we can find that time slips by, and we have not accomplished anything.

Even a project we know we will enjoy can fill us with a certain dread in anticipation. I have a pile of sewing projects sitting in a drawer, and once I manage to get going on them, I know they'll be done in a hurry. But somehow it's hard to get started. If we follow up promptly with our children when we assign them a job (overcoming our own inertia!), we can help them develop the habit of getting a job done quickly rather than sliding into procrastination.

If getting started is tough, finishing can be even

---

1. Pope John Paul II, *Laborem Exercens.*

90

tougher. We're all lazy in some areas, and if it's not housework, then it's spiritual growth, or generous service to parish or friends, or political affairs, or something else. And at one time or another we all—adults and children—are tempted to do just enough to get by. Or we may be sidetracked by interruptions before we have a chance to finish a job. The end result of all these factors is that we, and our children, do not experience the satisfaction of completing a job. We do our children a service if we teach them to stick with a job and enjoy the satisfaction that comes with getting it squared away.

We can contribute to our children's enjoyment of work at home by allowing them the satisfaction of doing a job from start to finish. I vividly remember sitting in my parents' kitchen chopping nuts, thinking how much I hated chopping nuts and how I wished I could be making the whole cake. Henry Ford invented the assembly line because it is more efficient: It is easier to train someone to do a specific part of a job than to teach each worker to do all the parts that make up the whole job. But efficiency is not the dominant consideration at home. Our children can develop a resistant feeling toward work if we limit them to tasks that don't provide an opportunity for them to grow.

We promote a sense of pride in our children by expecting them to do quality work. When I allow my children to half-clean their rooms, and get away with it, we all feel bad. I'm uncomfortable because I didn't follow through and because the room still looks terrible. They walk away without the satisfaction of having an orderly room. When I work with them and teach them to fold their clothes carefully and to find a good place for their stray things, we all feel happy. No one takes pride in doing a job badly if he or she is capable of doing it well. When we allow our children to do slipshod work we deprive them of one of the joys of work.

The best way for our children to learn to work well is for us to teach them. Schools, athletics coaches, and employers can teach our children some good work habits, but the job is best started at home.

We will do best if we consciously take the time to teach each child the process. This usually isn't a problem with the oldest child, but the rest of the children often have to shift for themselves. I carefully listed the items needed when my first child learned how to set the table, but when the job passed on to the second and third, I forgot that they didn't automatically realize that we need silverware as well as plates and glasses. Like many parents, I have to overcome the tendency to simply assign new jobs to younger children rather than teaching them.

An important aid in teaching our children to work is breaking the job into smaller steps, or structuring it to their needs. One day I gave my 3-year-old the job of picking up all the scraps of paper on the floor. She took one look at the mess and started wailing. Her idea of doing the job was to carry each piece of paper separately to the wastebasket in the kitchen. When I supplied her with a brown paper bag for collecting the paper, she cheered up and trotted around the room picking up scraps.

When teaching children to work, particularly to

do repetitious tasks like routine housework, we need to praise them—often and loudly. One of the disappointing aspects of homemaking is the lack of recognition and praise for our work, and surely we don't want to inflict the same misfortune on our children. The child who is a poor worker at home but who excels in athletics or schoolwork may do so because he or she gets the praise in these activities that is lacking at home. Expecting the best from our children, and delighting in it when it comes, has the power to uncover all sorts of good things in our children.

It is also important that our children feel there is some end to the work. I grew up in an enormous house with seven younger brothers and sisters, one of whom was profoundly retarded. As a child I felt there was no point in hurrying to finish a job, because there would always be another to do. I developed an attitude of passivity about housework which is still a hindrance to me today.

Building Relationships

Our family relationships are made up of many things: talking, eating meals, celebrating holidays—and working together. Working together has tremendous potential for strengthening family relationships. Working with others establishes a camaraderie which cannot be achieved any other way.

We recently put a new roof on our house, and my father and brothers and sisters came over to work.

They had told me how they enjoyed the other roofing projects they had done, but secretly I thought they were out of their minds. I had been content to send my husband to help with a pot of chili tucked under his arm. I spent the first day of our roofing project in the kitchen cooking for the crew, but on the second day my husband developed a sore back. He took over the cooking, and I went up on the roof. To my amazement, I thoroughly enjoyed the day: bantering about one another's expertise or lack of it, gasping as my brother strolled nonchalantly along the peak of the roof, and the lulls in the conversation when the silence was broken only by the ringing of hammers. It was a very special day.

We need to try to carry the fun of special projects into the day-to-day routine of work. Children love to watch adults working in the garage or at the workbench, and as they get older they enjoy being able to help. Baking Christmas cookies is a family ritual, and indeed cooking is always a good community project. Although the burden of work sometimes separates us from others, more often it allows us a unique opportunity to strengthen family relationships.

Our Work's Importance for Us

We cannot teach our children to take pride in their work unless we have pride in our own. Some women who found great satisfaction in their previous careers are hard pressed to see housework as a source of pride. In part, this is because homemakers have become separated from their work. For example, packaged foods are an important tool for saving precious time. But most products which save time also reduce the amount of skill required by the user. If we consistently relegate ourselves to the position of unskilled user, eventually we begin to feel the part.

If I offer someone a piece of cake made from a mix, I feel uncomfortable accepting any compliments on it. If someone comments favorably, my response is likely to be, "Oh, thanks, but it's just out of a box." We all know it's practically impossible to ruin a box cake unless you drop it on the floor, so few feel a particular sense of accomplishment in successfully making one. On the other hand we can really bask in the compliments if we bake a cake from scratch.

As in so many other areas of our lives, each of us will strike a different balance in the pride we take in our work. We get a whole array of mail-order catalogs geared to homesteaders, and I can't imagine ordering some of the equipment. The washtubs, for instance, which require the clothes to be stirred with a stick and then fed manually through a wringer, have absolutely no charm for me. Yet we have tried our hand attending chickens, rabbits, ducks, sheep and a one-third acre garden,and I've shoveled more manure than I care to think about. I still can't explain why I find the job satisfying.

Women who do not possess housekeeping skills often have the most difficult transition to becoming homemakers. If it's hard to feel proud of a box cake that turns out well, it's impossible to be happy about a scratch cake that turns out badly. And a whole succession of them is downright miserable. For years I hated sewing because I spent so much time ripping out sleeves I had put in backward, going to the store for elastic I forgot to buy, and so on. Once I struggled through enough projects to become fairly proficient, I began to enjoy sewing. Women who do not know how to cook or clean effectively will not be able to really enjoy being home until they develop those skills.

Few of us will be good at everything. I feel thoroughly embarrassed when someone who keeps a tidier house than I do drops in on me. And some women who keep lovely, clean houses feel intimidated by my homemade bread and hand-knit sweaters. It would be so much better if we could simply enjoy one another's gifts and make peace with our own limitations. We need to realistically appraise our performance, be happy about our strengths, and continue to work at our weak areas while not despairing of ourselves because of them.

There is an adjustment in attitude which can help us. Most people evaluate work in terms of its products. This approach to housework dooms us to frustration. Every single item I clean is destined to get dirty again—unless it breaks first. Everything I cook will be eaten (hopefully), and those carefully stitched overalls are going to get holes in the knees. If I see my work only in terms of its products—a clean floor, a good meal, a pair of overalls—then I am bound to become discouraged.

I sew for the results, and so I mutter to myself every time I have to rip out a seam. But there are some jobs I do just because I enjoy the process. I enjoy knitting simply because the mindless repetition is soothing; sweaters and mittens are only a bonus. When I have to unravel a sleeve because it's too big, I honestly don't mind—much.

As long as my goal is the product, though, I will feel defeated and angry when someone interferes with that goal. For instance, if my goal is to have a clean carpet, then I will feel happy immediately after it's vacuumed. But with four small children and a few dogs in a country house, the condition of the carpet and my disposition will deteriorate rapidly and simultaneously. If, on the other hand, I can set a *process* goal, to vacuum every day, or every other day, or once a week, then I have still accomplished my goal even when the carpet is less than perfectly clean. If someone drops in unexpectedly, I may still squirm a little, but in my heart I know I met my goal, and my self-esteem isn't quite as threatened. Process goals help us cope with the wear and tear a family inevitably puts on a house.

Taking care of something also gives us a sense that it belongs to us. We moved into our present home in late summer and did not have any equipment to work the land. The weeds on the place had grown up to our necks, and it was hard even to walk to the far end of the property. I spent the winter making plans for where we would fence the pasture and how we would plant the garden, but I didn't feel that we really *owned* the land until the following spring when we could start putting some of our plans into effect and I actually tramped back and forth over the ground.

Technically our house belongs to us because we make our mortgage payments and somebody someplace has the deed in storage for us. But personally, I feel the house belongs to me because I painted the kitchen cupboards and washed the windows. When I let the closets get messy and the curtains dingy, I feel a sense of distance between the house and me; I shut the door quickly when I pull a sheet out of the closet and try to shut the problem out of my thoughts. But when I've just cleaned the place, I feel that it's really mine, and I am thrilled that I can claim it.

In a similar way, homemaking brings us closer to our families. Of course we don't own people, but when I brush my daughter's hair and put ribbons in it, I become especially aware that she's "my" little girl. The work we do for our families gives them the pleasure of being cared for, and gives us all a greater feeling of belonging.

Furthermore, our physical work can provide an outlet for excess psychic energy. Marriage and childrearing have their built-in frustrations, and a bout of housecleaning can burn up some adrenalin that might get put to some less useful purpose. Some people run around the block to blow off steam; a Benedictine Sister I know used to scrub the walls of her apartment when the frustrations of working on her doctorate got to her. I've never been driven to such lengths, but sometimes I do my best housecleaning when I'm mad. It wouldn't be my outlet of first choice, but given a shortage of alternatives it has its merits. Work shouldn't be used as a means of avoiding conflict, but it can help us keep from blowing things out of proportion.

It's not only negative energy that can be used up with housework. Given a chance, I could talk all day long—but my husband certainly couldn't. My children are little enough now that they still delight in my company, but I know the day will come when school and friends will take up most of their time. For those of us without outside jobs, housework can constructively use up some energy that might otherwise be pumped into unrealistic expectations of family relationships.

Toward a Theology of Work

The first chapters of the book of Genesis hold many profound truths about human existence, and the role of work in our lives is among them. Whether we understand the early books of the Bible literally or poetically, the essential message remains the same. When God put Adam and Eve in the garden, he did not tell them, "Go sit around in the garden and relax." Rather, he commanded them to "fill the earth and conquer it" (Gn 1:28). The garden was the place of perfect human happiness—and yet Adam and Eve worked there. Without the presence of sin, God's command to work was pure gift, a joyful exercise of talents.

We can catch a glimpse of what work could be like if we observe little children. As soon as infants are old enough to stay awake for any length of time, they begin the work of learning about their environments. Once they can creep, they spend hours every day earnestly exploring everything within reach. They love to laugh and play, but watching their sober little faces as they struggle to climb onto a chair or carefully take a flashlight apart, we can see that they take these activities very seriously indeed. Contrast the joy with which they perform the phenomenal feat of mastering the English language with your own memories of French, German or Spanish classes! Without sin, our experience of work would be very much like a child's. Although work would require effort, we would exult in our capacity to do it.

Whether or not we believe that original sin was committed by two specific people and passed on by them to the human race, we can agree on its effects. Original sin is the name for the disorder that exists within us, the "I do not do the good that I wish to do" that St. Paul speaks of. Because of sin, we are alienated from ourselves, from God, from one another, from all of creation. And we are tragically alienated from our work. God's curse to Adam and Eve focuses heavily on work:

> "Accursed be the soil because of you.
> With suffering shall you get your food from it
> every day of your life.
> It shall yield you brambles and thistles,
> and you shall eat wild plants.
> With sweat on your brow
> shall you eat your bread,
> until you return to the soil,
> as you were taken from it" (Gn 3:17-19).

The boredom, fatigue and rebellion we feel against

100

work is a result of sin, and not in the nature of work
itself.

It is our task to restore wholeness to our relationship with God, ourselves and other people. An integral part of this struggle is the challenge of reconciling ourselves to our work. Children give us a glimpse
of the exultant joy possible in work, but as adults we
will feel that surge of satisfaction only intermittently.
We must cope with our own distaste for work, and
strive to rediscover its proper role in our lives.

When we seek out the proper role of work in our
lives, we are sharing in Jesus' act of redemption.
Through his death and resurrection, Jesus redeemed
us all—he made it possible for us to come back to
wholeness. The fundamental purpose of our lives is to
accept that redemption and to allow its power to
transform every aspect of our lives. An integral part of
this struggle is the challenge of reconciling ourselves
with work. Achieving wholeness is a lifelong project,
as we slowly discover the disorder within us and the
astounding freedom that comes from moving out of
that darkness into light. As we become whole through
our work, we extend that redemption to yet another
portion of our lives.

Disorder extends even to the natural world. St.
Paul has told us that *all* creation has been redeemed
through Christ. Isaiah describes the harmony of the
new creation:

> The wolf lives with the lamb,
> the panther lies down with the kid,
> calf and lion cub feed together

with a little boy to lead them.
The cow and the bear make friends,
their young lie down together (Is 11:6-7).

When we stumble across our bedroom, tripping over toys, unable to find any clean underwear, we are coping with a disordered world. When we achieve the right balance of organization for our homes, we restore order and harmony, qualities of a redeemed creation. By caring for our homes properly, we provide the best possible environments in which to find ourselves, one another, and God.

By our work, we not only share in the redemptive action of Jesus, but we also take part in the Father's creative act. According to Genesis, God created the universe out of chaos. Spend a few days sick in bed, and it quickly becomes apparent that our starting point is the same. As God shaped that chaos into a shining world, so we too can bring the elements around us to life.

Young children are fascinated by just how God made the world, and their questions can be difficult to answer.

"Did God make the sky?"
"Of course."
"Did God make the trees?"
"Yes."
"Did God make our house?"
"Well, um. . . ."

God did create the world, and he holds us all in existence. But he left his creation incomplete, and chose to depend on us to continue his creative process. We do not create tomatoes, but God allows us to plant seeds, to water and weed the plant, and to take pride in the first ripe fruit. We have the privilege of sharing in his creation.

God simply spoke the word, and the world was made. We need to work hard to bring our dreams into reality. I have a vision of what I hope for my kitchen: sun streaming through clean windows, freshly baked muffins steaming on a checked tablecloth beside a mug filled with fresh flowers. But it is only through a lot of physical work that I can translate that dream into reality. Physical work is the means by which we incarnate our love for one another. We give it physical substance so that it can touch others' senses—warm and feed and comfort them—and thus touch their hearts.

The New Testament parable of the talents reaffirms the importance of work. A master gave three servants varying amounts of money, expecting them to invest and multiply it. The servants who put the money to work were rewarded, while the servant who was too frightened to take any risks was punished. God has given each of us talents, but unless we work with them we too may be called to account. Our talents do not simply lie dormant when they are not exercised—gradually they are lost to us. It is only by our work that we bring our talents to fruition.

Sometimes we fail to see the value of our physical work. We tend to assume that mental work is somehow superior. If that's so, then God is terribly inefficient. It's always puzzled me, for instance, that God created us to live only about 70 years on earth, and then designed us so that we spend about 20 of those years sleeping. And most of our waking time must be spent taking care of our physical needs. Surely this is a waste of time—unless God, too, sees our physical life as having importance.

Our work is made easier if we find a balance of physical and mental activities. Someone who works at a desk job all day may be refreshed by a brisk walk, or even by pushing a lawnmower. I read about a writer who spent many fruitless hours staring at his typewriter when he was pursuing a writing career full time. After he got a part-time job as a tree cutter, he found he produced many more finished pages while devoting substantially less time to the effort. The physical work balanced his mental efforts and made them more productive. I'll never enjoy cleaning a refrigerator in the same way that I enjoy raking the lawn on the first sunny day of spring, but both jobs are part of the balance of physical and mental activities in my life.

Gratitude for God's many gifts requires that we care for them properly. If we gave a lovely sweater to a friend and discovered she wore it to clean out her garage, we would feel that she did not really value the gift. Our homes, our clothing, our cars and the food we have in such abundance are all gifts that have not been given to most of the world's population. We are called to care for them well—and share them generously.

Our culture promotes an incredible amount of waste. We are so surrounded by it that we are not even aware it exists. The only people I know, for instance, who turn out lights when they leave a room are a Cambodian refugee family still unaccustomed to the luxury of electricity. Our children lose jackets and leave bikes out in the rain. There are people who have dramatized American wastefulness by living for weeks on meals fished out of other people's garbage. Abundance seems to lead to carelessness, and we have all been abundantly blessed. Our homemaking tasks are aimed at caring for the gifts we have been given, and when we serve up those leftovers as attractively as possible, or attack a stain before it has a chance to set, we are acting as good stewards.

Our time is also a precious gift from God. To steward it well, we will not waste it on unnecessary housekeeping jobs. Part of the challenge of good homemaking is striking the proper balance: keeping our houses clean and charming, our meals tasty and our clothes attractive, without forgetting that those gifts are only temporary.

Work is a gift which, like many others, requires moderation. Many of us feel guilty if we're not always working. Our society has not taught us a proper balance between work and leisure. The *workaholic*, the person addicted to work, is a common phenomenon. And yet many other people see work only as the necessary evil required to land a paycheck. TGIF (Thank God It's Friday) limps a little as a philosophy of life, particularly if you work homemakers' hours.

If home is the ideal place to learn about work, it is also the best place to learn about leisure. God rested on the Sabbath and invites us to do the same. Indeed, the traditional observance of Sunday contains the two vital elements which balance work in our lives: rest and prayer.

The Christian life is a blend of action and contemplation. In the past, the action was left to the lay people and contemplation belonged to the Carmelites. As lay people take on more leadership in the church, we would do well to also learn more about contemplation. Hyperactivity is one of the most common barriers to a solid prayer life. If we spend all our time in activity, we begin to think that rather than share in Jesus' redemption, we can substitute for it. Recreation refreshes us; prayer gives us direction.

No matter how much we respect our work, or how efficient we become, an element of pain will always be with us. Physical pain in housework is rare, perhaps an occasional scorched finger or aching back, but psychologically housework takes a toll. Pain of any sort can be either debilitating or transforming, and it is up to us to decide whether the pain in our lives will weaken or strengthen us.

Of the seven deadly sins, pride was named as our point of greatest vulnerability. My father says that the Lord does not send humility, he sends humiliation. To be more precise, he sends the grace to grow from humiliation, and as homemakers we have plenty of opportunities to be graced.

Our house has a little bathroom, with a toilet wedged into a narrow recess between the sink and the wall. Something in me rebels against squeezing headfirst into that tiny area to scrub behind the toilet. I hate grubbing around on my knees in the back of the closet searching for my child's stray socks. Those jobs seem somehow demeaning. All homemakers have at one time or another wanted to shriek, "I'm not your slave, I'm a person!"

It is very important for our families' sakes that they not see us as their servants. At the same time, it is valuable for us to remember that we are. St. Paul writes about Jesus:

> His state was divine,
> yet he did not cling
> to his equality with God but emptied himself
> to assume the condition of a slave,
> and became as men are;
> and being as all men are,
> he was humbler yet,
> even to accepting death,
> death on a cross (Phil 2:6-8).

We want people to remember that we have talents, and it's right that we feel that way. At the same time, in a paradoxical reality that we come to understand only through living it, we are called to let go of our "higher" talents and to empty ourselves for others.

Humility is a true understanding of who we are: God's creatures, flawed yet marvelous. There is nothing wrong with scrubbing toilets and as long as I feel that there is I have not properly understood myself. The Christian journey is one of discovery: We discover our gifts and then we learn how to give them away. The inevitably humbling aspects of our job provide us with ample opportunity to begin this mysterious process.

We said earlier that God's will for us is revealed in the needs of those to whom we are committed. My children need their noses wiped and their beds changed when they're sick at 2 a.m. I don't like doing those things, and I may do them simply because I can't get out of them. To the extent that I do my work grudgingly, I am likely to feel trapped and resentful. But if I believe that God has a plan for me, and that right now his plan includes all this messy work, then I can choose to accept my lot out of obedience to his will. An enormous freedom comes when I take my life in my two hands and say to the Lord, "I accept your will for me." The work is the same, but I have changed.

When I heard Mother Teresa of Calcutta speak several years ago, a person in a wheelchair asked her what he could do to help her work. Mother Teresa looked straight at him and invited him to offer his sufferings for her. She and her workers rely heavily on the prayers and sufferings of many people for the strength they need to continue their efforts at serving the poor.

Sometimes when I'm feeling sorry for myself, I think of the millions of women in the world whose lives are so much more difficult than mine. They are the women who have no houses to keep clean, who carry their water in jugs on their heads, sleep on the ground when they're pregnant and watch their children die of malnutrition. When I think of them, I realize that my own frustrations are trivial in comparison. The thought of their suffering puts my own into perspective, and I offer whatever is bothering me at the time to unite me with them and ask God's blessing on them. Pain, much as it frightens us, is a valuable resource, and one we often waste. Freely offered to God, united with Jesus' suffering, it truly has the power to redeem.

Special times

We've talked about *people* in each chapter, and Chapters 3 and 4 discussed *place* at length. Now we will deal with the third precious commodity with which homemakers work: *time.*

Ask a random group of people in the business world what time it is, and I doubt that you would find one who could not give you a precise answer. They live on clock time. When I was teaching, I reported to school at 7:45 a.m. and left at 3:30 p.m. with about two hours' worth of evening work tucked under my arm. When my job required extra effort, I received tidy memos in my mailbox informing me of the time and place. If I needed to discuss a course or a student with another teacher, I set up an appointment. I was often frantically busy, but I knew where I was to be when. If either my husband or I felt the absolute need for a break, we could block out some specific time to relax and unwind. I felt some sort of control over my life.

But ask a group of homemakers the time, and many will not be wearing watches. We tucked them away in drawers when we became homemakers.

The first baby brings an explosive disruption of

our time. The first clue usually comes as we wait to go into labor. A due date is simply something we use to pacify ourselves; babies come when they please. After they arrive, they intend to eat when they are hungry and be held when they are lonely. They live on biological time. Not only have they never seen a clock, they don't even know the difference between night and day. The new parents, accustomed to planning their days and eating and sleeping on schedule—clock time—usually feel as though their lives have been wrenched out of their hands by the tiny little body they have brought home from the hospital. Those lovable little chunks of humanity turn our worlds upside down. A dramatic lowering of our expectations of life (simple survival is about right) helps get us through those first few months. Teaching the baby the difference between night and day is first on the agenda, and the first unbroken night's sleep is a milestone.

Babies gradually settle into some semblance of a routine, but their schedule is rhythmical rather than structured. Children live largely on biological time for many years, and many of our conflicts with them come as we try to fit them into clock time. A prime time for losing our tempers with children is when we are struggling to meet a deadline. Packing the kids into snowsuits, boots and mittens for a doctor's appointment, or cleaning the house in time for company, is likely to reduce me to hysterics. The morning ritual of hustling kids off to school can be a battleground right through college for some families. It takes many years for children to learn to submit to the demands of clock time.

For the mother who is home full time with the baby, the abrupt transition from clock time to biological time can produce bewilderment, panic, and sometimes anger. We often feel as though we have lost all control over our lives, and that our freedom has vanished. That is not really the case.

Even homemakers with young children have a fair amount of free time. But the time comes unpredictably and in snatches. When a bit of free time magically appears, we have to shift gears quickly so we can enjoy it before it disappears. If somehow, unexpectedly, all the children are sleeping or otherwise occupied, I drop the broom and grab a book or my sewing. Fifteen minutes later the normal chaos erupts again and I have to stop, but I know another 15 minutes will appear later. The time we need is available, but we won't discover it as long as we're trying to operate on clock time. We need to let go of our old dependence on predictable, uninterrupted free time and learn to flow with the rhythm of biological time. It's like learning to swim: If I try to walk from the shallow end to the deep end of a pool, I will surely drown. But if I can trust the water, letting go of the security of having my feet on something solid, I can travel effectively.

Homemakers with children in school often spend much of their time chauffeuring, which can be even more fragmenting than caring for preschoolers. They, and women who have jobs or are involved in other demanding outside activities, must live on clock time and biological time simultaneously. We all need to develop and then retain that ability to recognize and to use spare moments for activities that re-create us.

It took me several years to adjust to living comfortably on biological time. For instance, when I'm pregnant I am often awake for two or three hours in the middle of the night. Since I know that "normal" people sleep at night and are awake during the day, I used to stare at the ceiling over my bed at 3 a.m. and then stagger around exhausted the next day. Finally, toward the end of my fourth pregnancy I realized that there is nothing sacred about sleeping only at night. I could get up at 3 a.m. and do some quiet housework, or anything else that can be done in a foggy state, and then nap during the day. Insomnia seems to be a common affliction of homemakers, and life can be easier if we take advantage of the fact that we are not bound to the clock as are most other workers.

What mother has not spent a sleepless night with a sick child? If we allow ourselves the slow start we deserve the next morning, a neighbor may catch us at 10 a.m. in our bathrobe. Even though we know we have every right to be breakfasting at 10 a.m., we are usually embarrassed to be seen padding around the house undressed. People are "supposed" to be in street clothes by 10 a.m. When we finally recognize that our timetable is not the same as other workers', we can take the most sensible and comfortable action for our circumstances.

In addition to the freedom, there are other advantages to living on biological time. More than most other workers, we can live in tune with the seasons. In our technological society, we are largely buffered from the effects of the seasons. My husband gamely slogs through the snow to work in winter, following the massive plows which clear pathways within hours of a 12-inch snowstorm. He arrives at his heated office which has no windows to show him the glistening snow outside. The electricity lighting his office disregards the fluctuation in day length. In summer, his office is air-conditioned, protecting him from the sweltering heat and filtering out any excess humidity.

Homemakers, too, can hermetically seal the house and sail through the year disregarding the changes in nature. But those homemakers living in areas with a change of seasons have the opportunity to enjoy the rhythms of the year. Our Minnesota winters are long and cold. I enjoy the coziness of early winter, making the house snug as the leaves fall and the snow begins to drift. But February and March are simply awful; one child or another has been coughing since September, and our time outside and our visits with other people have been minimal. As a result, *nobody* enjoys spring like we do. I remember sitting in our back yard a few years ago on that first warm day of spring, watching our neighbors' horses chasing each other around the pasture. They, the kids and I were all bursting with spring fever, and I felt sorry for my husband in his weatherproof office.

The homemaker who is in tune with the seasons can bring her house into harmony with them as well. My aunt has a winter furniture arrangement, and a summer one. In the winter she aims for cozy: She moves the furniture toward the center of the room and brings out all her knickknacks. During the summer she clears the shelves and moves the furniture out to the walls, creating an open and airy feeling.

In praise of homemaking

Creating Special Times

I'll be home for Christmas, you can plan on
me.
Please have snow and mistletoe and presents
on the tree.
Christmas Eve will find me where the lovelight
gleams.
I'll be home for Christmas, if only in my
dreams.[1]

The haunting wistfulness of that song stems from
the very special emotions that Christmas calls up in
each of us. "Christmas spirit" is a combination of excitement, nostalgia, anticipation and warmth that is
unmatched by any other.

How is it that the Christmas season has come to
be the high point of the year for so many people? The
day itself can be anti-climactic for many adults, and
the press of last-minute shopping may be absolutely
miserable. We know that often the birth of Jesus gets
lost in the hoopla; indeed, many people's enthusiasm
for Christmas has nothing at all to do with the birth of
our Savior. But shining lights strung along a porch
roof, and the glow through a window of a multi-
colored Christmas tree, touch memories of childhood
Christmases and make us want to re-create the
magic.

Christmas has become so important because
people have worked to make it so. The church, the
retailers, and families, all with very different motives,
have put tremendous effort into making it a
memorable time of year. For Christian families,

1. "I'll Be Home for Christmas." Copyright © 1948, 1956 by Kim
Gannon-Walter Kent, Hollywood, CA. All rights reserved. Used by permission of the copyright owner.

Christmas is significant because it heightens our awareness of God's action in our lives and brings us closer to those we love.

Christmas is a great case study for homemakers wanting to discover the elements that go into creating special times at home. Like the important places in our lives, special times in our lives tie us emotionally to the people and values that are central to us. Creating special *time* is as fundamental to homemaking as creating a special *place*. Let's take a look at some of the elements involved in making Christmas: music, decorations, food, religious practices and gifts.

Retailers pipe Christmas music into the stores in October because they know that hearing carols will get us into the mood of Christmas—and we will start buying. Christmas music may be the only music that bridges the gap among all generations, which is one reason we enjoy it so much. Our favorite carols are the oldest: "Silent Night," "O Come All Ye Faithful," "What Child Is This?" Advent hymns such as "O Come, O Come Emmanuel" link us to our distant past recalling the Jews longing for the coming of the Messiah. We can sing these hymns with our grandparents, as they sang them with theirs. People who haven't sung a note all year still enjoy gathering around a piano to sing carols at Christmas.

Decorating the house is central to Christmas. Who can imagine Christmas without a Christmas tree? People traveling at Christmas have even been known to lug two-foot pines into their hotel rooms. Red, green and white, the colors we associate with Christmas, are everywhere. Wreaths and candles, poinsettias and holly, wrapped gifts and colored lights speak Christmas to us from every room of the house. In many homes the Nativity set occupies a special place, waiting for the figure of the Christ child to be added on Christmas eve.

Christmas cookies, fruitcakes and festive drinks also mark our celebration of the Christmas season. Christmas dinner usually presents dishes which have become traditional in the family. Good food is another part of the Christmas spirit.

Churches that stand half-empty throughout the year are packed at Christmas. Even people who never crack open a bible enjoy listening to the Christmas story.

Gifts are a sign of Christmas; at their best, they express our joy at Jesus' presence among us and our gratitude at being given so many people to love.

Christmas isn't the most important feast in our religious year, but most of us behave as though it were. We probably get more involved in celebrating Christmas than in any other event in our lives, except perhaps marriage. Christmas is a prime example of what effective celebration can do: The warm memories and the gathering of families are among the things that make us most happy to be human.

But to be whole our families need not just one, but many special times throughout the year. The elements that make the celebrations of Christmas distinctive can also be used to create other important moments in our families' histories. The special times we create at home fall roughly into three categories: those which celebrate the individuals in our families, those which celebrate the family itself, and those which celebrate broader elements like our faith community or our country.

The most obvious way most families honor individuals is by celebrating birthdays. Birthdays are a time to remember how precious each person is, and how grateful we are that God has given him or her to us. Young children start to count the days until their birthday weeks ahead of time. The day is special because we receive gifts, of course, but also because it is *our* day.

Some families have a "red plate special" tradition. They buy a red dinner plate and have "You are special" written on it. Then, whenever someone in the family has a success—Dad's raise, Karen's soccer goal, Mark's high score in algebra—the red plate is set to mark the occasion.

In our family we also try to celebrate baptismal anniversaries and name days. We're still a little haphazard at remembering, but we're working to establish the tradition. Surely our baptism, the day which marks our reception into the family of Christians, is a day worth remembering. We burn the child's baptismal candle and have a special dinner.

On name days we read something about the life of the patron saint. Everyone needs heroes, and good ones are hard to come by these days. We need to hear about people who have lived whole, victorious lives in this broken world. What more suitable heroes can we propose to our children than those who have served God so faithfully?

The recent trend in biography is toward digging up the "dirt" on people. This is disillusioning for us all. It's not necessary to ignore the saints' imperfections to be inspired by them; in fact, sometimes it's reassuring to remember that they could get just as ornery as we do. Saints, too, have dirt on their faces, but they succeeded because they didn't allow that dirt to obscure their vision of God.

Some family traditions are developed deliberately, but many just happen. We have neighbors who spend much of each summer at a family cottage. Over the years many hours were spent on their tennis court in friendly competition with the family next door. By the time the children were adults an annual tournament had developed with family members making the trip from as far away as South America to attend. The families publish a booklet with fictitious accounts of each player's prowess, and have an elaborate food and maintenance schedule. What began as simple tennis games has become a powerful magnet, drawing two families annually back to their centers.

When I was growing up, we often acted out the many story records we had at home. I remember coming home with a date one evening and walking in on a full-blown production of *Peter Pan,* with my mother mouthing Wendy Darling's words to my sister's Peter Pan. I didn't know whether to be embarrassed or proud.

We also had regular family nights with a standard menu of pizza, popcorn and malts. After the pizza and popcorn we would spread our pillows and quilts on the floor in front of the fireplace, turn out the lights, put on records, and bask in the coziness. The first time my husband and I had pizza after our marriage, he was appalled when I started popping corn, and I was amazed that anyone would eat pizza without it. That's one tradition that didn't survive the transition from the Fourré family to the Zimney family.

The Mormons have a strong tradition of family nights. Whatever the ages of the children living at home, one evening a week is kept free of outside activities. Families have some discussion, some fun, and some goodies. The Mormons have published resource books on family nights for those who would like to make the evening one for faith-sharing as well as family togetherness.

Sundays have great potential as family days. Few schools or churches schedule activities on Sunday afternoons or evenings. Although older children's work schedules pose a problem, Sunday is still probably the easiest time for families to appropriate for themselves.

Games form an important part of many families' traditions. My sister and her husband play board games with their preschool children almost every evening during the winter. Other families work jigsaw puzzles or play touch football. Some games are especially fun because they're so absurd. Sardines, one of our favorites, is a form of hide-and-seek best played in the dark. One person hides, and as each person finds her, he squeezes with her into the hiding place. The last "seeker" may find a bathtub crammed full of giggling players. There are many resource books available with ideas for family games and crafts.

Families also develop their own styles of cooking. My mother is a great bread baker, and my sisters and I carry on the tradition. A cousin called me recently for a recipe, and when I didn't have it she asked in mock disgust, "What's the use of being a Fourré if you don't know how to make almond rolls?"

Ethnic cooking can be an important part of a family's tradition. Immigrants will adopt a country's language and clothing long before they give up their native cooking. The success of Ragu spaghetti sauce's advertising slogan, "Aah, that's Italian!" depends heavily on the image of the Italian family crowded together around the table enjoying "real" Italian food. Restaurants advertise home-style meals, and home cooking is one of the things young people often miss most when they leave home.

Every family has favorite foods that it enjoys together. It may be as simple as an evening bowl of popcorn or as unpredictable as popovers. Cooking together is also a great family activity, especially if we're working to produce one of our specialties. We are not simply producing the food which disappears in minutes; we are also creating memories that last a lifetime.

We celebrate family life more formally in events such as weddings, anniversaries and funerals. Family life isn't always glorious, and we need to take time out occasionally to remind ourselves of the good times. Despite the often frantic and trying preparations, the beauty and serenity of the wedding ceremony, for example, express all our deepest hopes for the couple, and at every wedding we remember the hope-filled day when we began the adventure of our own marriage.

Anniversaries too are a time to reminisce, to remember the funny moments and the sad ones. With all our quirks, we have come a long way together, and in spite of our difficulties our families have made us the people we are today.

Funerals, strange as it seems, are special celebrations of family, too. The tradition of assembling at the time of death gives us a sense of perspective, of where the person we have lost fits into the whole scheme of family. We are made powerfully aware of what a person's presence has meant to us and how his or her absence will affect us. Surrounded by relatives, some of whom we see only at funerals, we are also reminded of the bonds of kinship among those who remain.

Like a good photo, family celebrations and traditions capture something of the essence of our families' characters and etch them firmly into our hearts and memories. Our job as homemakers is to recognize established traditions and those in the making, and to be willing to commit ourselves to helping them spread their richness through the fabric of our family life.

Faith

The church helps us celebrate the important elements in our lives through the sacraments. But she also provides tremendous resources for us to make real the abiding truths of our faith: God's love for us, our need for healing, the redemptive action of the Son, and the presence of the Spirit. The cycle of the church year, especially the high points of Christmas,

Easter and Pentecost, reflects the ever-present rhythms of our lives.

By temperament and upbringing, we tend to be more at home with one type of spiritual experience than another. Some of us are born penitents, always aware of our own sinfulness. Others feel contentedly supported by God's love and secure in his forgiveness. Still others are inclined to forget the whole thing. The liturgical year helps us round out any natural imbalance we may have. Advent is a time for longing and listening, for being aware of God's wonderful promises. Lent is housecleaning time. Pentecost reminds us of the transforming power of the Spirit. As we enter into the church's celebration of the liturgical year, we can develop those aspects of spirituality where our awareness is dim.

We lose much of the impact of the church year if we encounter it only at church. It is by bringing the seasons of the year into our homes that we can really live them. God cannot be touched or heard directly, and since we are people with eyes and ears and fingers, we need to find ways in which our senses can help us encounter him. Our belief in God will have little impact on our lives unless our hearts are touched.

If we want to pass our faith on to our children, it is essential that we make life with God *concrete* for them. Celebrating the liturgical year at home is a wonderful way of doing that.

Advent is a favorite time of year for me. My sisters and brothers and I were brought up with a wealth of Advent traditions. Besides the traditional Advent wreath, we always made plum pudding on the first Sunday of Advent. I secretly thought the pudding tasted terrible when we ate it at Christmas, but I loved mashing all those ingredients together at the beginning of Advent. It was a ritual, and children love rituals.

We also had a cradle for Jesus which we softened throughout Advent by placing a straw in it for each good deed. We hung symbols for the biblical prophecies about Jesus (Star of David, Root of Jesse, etc.) on the bare branch of our Jesse tree. My children also love Advent because we have kept those traditions and added a few of our own.

Decorations, such an important part of Christmas, can help us celebrate the church's other seasons. When I think of Advent, I think of a quiet Bethlehem, Isaiah speaking his promises to all the world, shepherds watching their flocks under a starry sky, and our straw-filled cradle at home. A little scrambled historically, but the elements are there.

We generally think of decorations as joyful rather than somber, and since the old custom of covering crucifixes and statues during Passiontide has fallen by the wayside, finding a way to create a Lenten atmosphere presents something of a challenge. Banners, mobiles, candles and flowers can help bring the purple of Lent, the white of Easter and the red of Pentecost into our homes and help us constantly and quietly be aware of the events we celebrate.

Along with many other changes brought about by Vatican II, there have been sweeping changes in church music. The upshot is that we do not have an obvious musical tradition to draw on in celebrating life with God at home. When I was growing up we struggled through "At the Cross Her Station Keeping" as we did the stations of the cross at home because *everybody* sang that song during stations. I have no idea what we'll sing when the children get older, or whether we'll do the stations at all. But I do know that just as Christmas is enriched by carols, so our Lents and Easters and Pentecosts will benefit from appropriate musical traditions that we can enjoy together at home.

Traditional foods add to our feeling of celebration. Why should sticking a bunch of candles on a birthday cake make us feel special? But it does. We have specific foods that we serve on given days: perhaps colored eggs and ham at Easter, cranberries at Christmas, hot cross buns during Lent, pancakes on Shrove Tuesday. Many people of European or South American descent have elaborate food rituals to mark the feasts of the year and incorporating some of these in our family calendar can help us make each season more distinctive.

From families to nations, we set aside special times to celebrate together. Our celebrations help us define who we are and remind us of our goals while at the same time strengthening our bonds to one another. Important occasions in many cultures are marked by feasting. Thanksgiving Day has lost much of its original meaning as a time to thank God for our blessings and become more of a national holiday like the fourth of July. What Thanksgiving Day seems to mean now to most Americans is *turkey*! The army even ships tons of turkey to American troops overseas, because turkey dinner with all the trimmings, even if it's served in a mess hall, somehow takes the edge off the misery of spending the holiday thousands of miles from home. It puts us in touch with all our previous Thanksgiving celebrations and thus with our families and our feelings about home and country.

Teaching Moments

Traditions provide ideal opportunities for teaching our children about God. When our oldest child was just beginning to talk, I worried about how to teach him about God. I couldn't quite imagine having formal catechism lessons, but it seemed that the subject of God didn't arise as often as I would have liked. And the things I wanted to tell him about God seemed so abstract. As he got older he began to ask questions about God, much to my relief. But it is in our celebrations of the church year that we make some of our best contacts.

The Christmas story is an obvious vehicle for teaching children about God's love, and it is a story we delight in telling. But the Passover meal, which our family celebrates on Holy Thursday, is also an opportunity to present another of God's mighty acts in our history. The book of Exodus tells us,

> And when your children ask you, "What does this ritual mean?" you will tell them, "It is the sacrifice of the Passover in honor of Yahweh who passed over the houses of the sons of Israel in Egypt, and struck Egypt but spared our houses" (Ex 12:26-27).

An important part of the traditional Jewish Passover is the ceremonial questions asked by the children. And the foods used in the meal—salt water representing tears, bitter herbs representing hardship, ground apples and cinnamon symbolizing brick-making materials—have served for thousands of years as an occasion for explaining God's magnificent delivery of the Jews from slavery.

Rituals—doing certain things at certain times in certain ways—crop up everywhere. Little children have a bedtime ritual they insist on observing, and woe betide the parents who try to put them to bed minus their drinks or kisses! There are athletic rituals: cheerleaders all dressing alike and bouncing around in unison, the pre-game huddle, the applause as basketball players file into the gym. There is a ritual about the beginning of a musical performance, when the gradually dimming lights and the sound of the orchestra tuning up put us in a mood of anticipation. Rituals are an important part of our lives; we should not leave them to the secular world. Children love rituals because they provide the important feeling of belonging to a group.

Monotony is one of the hazards of homemaking. With so much repetition in our daily routine, we need to have a feeling that today is not the same as yesterday, that this week is different from the last and the next. Our celebrations lift us out of the grayness of our routine and put us back in touch with the really important elements of our lives.

The special times we create can also pull family members, at least momentarily, out of the whirlwind of their outside activities. The frantic pace that many families keep, between jobs, school and social activities, can prevent them from having a really common experience. It does no good to keep children home for a family night if all we do is stare at one another across the living room. We must balance their football games and drama clubs and parties with times at home that are also fun and satisfying.

There is nothing magical in these traditions. We will not become better Christians simply because we have Advent calendars or hang purple around the house during Lent. Just as the wonder of Jesus' birth is lost almost as often as it is found through all the Yuletide celebrations, so also we can become too immersed in the practicalities of our traditions. But if our fussing and fixing is combined with a real effort to come closer to the Lord and conform with his will, then our traditions develop a power to move us toward him at times when we might otherwise not make the effort. And they are one of our most valuable resources for encouraging our children to be at home with us and with the Lord.

The homemaker's contribution to society

As we gain a better understanding of our job as homemakers we get new energy for our work, but not everyone shares our enthusiasm. Thirty years ago people pitied any woman past the age of 22 who was not home raising a family. Friends assumed that given the chance every woman would choose to be a homemaker.

Today the assumption is often reversed. "What is surprising in this day and age is that of the women who are married and living with their husbands, half still prefer to stay home by the hearth. There is something wrong with this."[1]

This attitude challenges us to look hard at ourselves. Instinctively we know our work is important for our families, but we also wonder whether we have any impact beyond our homes. Is the homemaker in fact serving the world as well as her family? The answer is a resounding yes.

---

1. Colette Dowling, *The Cinderella Complex* (New York: Summit Books, 1981), p. 40.

The Primal Sanities

If there's one thing American culture claims to promote it's diversity. We pride ourselves on our freedom of choice and our independent frontier spirit. And yet at the same time the herd impulse rules many aspects of our lives. Jeans are tight one year, baggy the next and completely out of style the following year. Social service careers were the goal of many young people 10 years ago; today the stampede is toward business and technology. Even people's choice of a pet is affected by fashion. The American Kennel Club's *Gazette* expressed concern that the current fad breeds—Chows, Sharpeis and Rott-weilers—are large, muscular dogs that the average owner is incapable of controlling. But people buy them because they're in style, and for some people the choice will be a disaster.

Societies benefit from diversity. A country whose economy depends on one major export can be ruined by falling prices or a crop failure. A society in which virtually everyone spends the day working in an of-fice, store or factory narrows its range of experience, and in so doing it is impoverished.

Rene Dubos wrote about what he called primal sanities. For thousands of years people lived close to the earth, depending on it for survival. We mentioned in Chapter 4 that our love for lakes, rivers, campfires and spring rains probably stems from those early days. Human lives were profoundly affected by the seasons. Last fall, munching on a cookie, I glanced out the window and saw a few fat squirrels scampering around preparing for winter. As I looked at their bulging cheeks and plump rumps I realized that the extra pounds we humans carry in winter may not be simply the result of too many Christmas cookies. For thousands of years winter meant scanty rations for people just as it still does for wild animals, and our bodies continue to try to protect us from a hungry March.

Dubos writes, "The secrets of life can often be reached not so much by what we learn as by what we half remember with the biological memory of the human species."[2] People busy with full-time jobs have very little time to be searching for those half-memories. But with all our busyness, homemakers live close to the basics of existence—those secrets of life. Our lives are immersed in the rhythms of birth, growth and death. We have more freedom to help a sick neighbor, to be conscious of God's marvelous creation as we watch a baby's first halting steps or enjoy the silence of a winter snowfall.

We need people to hold down those 40-hour-a-week jobs, but it's also important for society that some people are attuned to those primal sanities. Without them, we may lose sight of some of those secrets of life which give meaning to our days.

---

2. Rene Dubos, *A God Within* (New York: Charles Scribner's Sons, 1972), p. 62.

Balance and Integration

We tend to compartmentalize our lives. We go to church to take care of the spiritual part of ourselves. School develops us intellectually and, rather accidentally, socially. Sports and fitness classes develop physical skills. Piano or dance or ceramics classes touch our love for beauty. Most jobs, whether punching buttons in a checkout line or teaching electrical engineering in a university, use a narrow range of skills. Only at home are the parts of our lives integrated into a whole.

Teachers assume that studying and homework are first priorities in students' lives. Anyone looking at some high school teams' practice schedules knows that coaches are convinced that winning the next game or meet is most important. Bosses believe that employees' first responsibilities are to the company. Political and volunteer commitments swallow our time. All these things clamor to be number one, and it is only at home that we learn to fit the elements together. In a good home we use all our faculties: We work and pray, laugh and learn, argue and make up. Home provides a center where we can evaluate the elements in our lives and try to set sane priorities. Without a strong home to balance them, a job or a school play or friends are likely to take over the lives of children and parents alike.

Public Broadcasting Service did a documentary recently on divorced parents sharing the custody of their young children. The children's lives were a flurry of activities, shuttling back and forth from one parent to the other, from babysitters to school to ballet lessons. The children got plenty of affection from their parents, but they had no center. Their lives looked like smorgasbords—all the necessary ingredients were available, but nobody had given them a plate to carry their food. As I watched them pack their suitcases each weekend to shift houses, the plentiful parts did not seem to equal a whole. Simone Weil has said, "To be rooted is perhaps the most important and least recognized need of the human soul."[3] A solid home provides fertile ground for setting down those roots.

Not only do churches, schools and jobs fail to integrate our lives, in many places they are also becoming less personal. Many parishes today are so large that people worship on Sunday morning surrounded by strangers. The one-room schoolhouse is long gone; instead students are bused to sleek new schools holding thousands of young people. Children can make friends during the fall quarter and then never see their new friends the following quarter because of class schedule changes. Companies are merging, and the loyalty and sense of belonging many people felt in a small company is lost as they become faceless numbers in a vast conglomerate.

If the home is simply a place where busy people nod in passing, it offers no refuge from the impersonality of larger places; but if it is a spot in which people are invested, then it provides a secure base for launching out into the bewildering excitement of other worlds.

3. Simone Weil, *The Need for Roots* (New York: Harper & Row, 1952), p. 43.

Counterculture

It's not enough simply to provide a place where family members can coordinate the various parts of their lives. We can't just bring home the pieces and then fit the jigsaw puzzle together. Some of the pieces need to be thrown away, because not everything offered to us out there is good.

It's difficult to choose a different path—to make choices which steer us away from the values we see in advertising and on television and which may separate us from our friends. But as Christians and even as human beings it is essential that we reject some of the values promoted by American culture.

Ten or 15 years ago we heard a lot about countercultures. Young people said that American society was a mess and they set up communes devoted to cooperation and a less materialistic lifestyle. Few of those communities remain, but they were based on a sound principle: There is strength in numbers. It's hard for us to be faithful to God's call when we must do it alone. A supportive community helps us to recognize our own call and to have the stamina to live it out. A family, rooted in a Christian home, is the first and most basic Christian community.

Americans tend to be hyperactive and nowhere is this more evident than among families with children in junior and senior high school. Children race from school to gymnastics, from jobs to hockey games. Homemakers are active with volunteer work or friends, and many parents have jobs which demand long hours away from home. Families with older children often find they don't have one meal a week where every family member is present.

When our society was largely agricultural, families spent most of their time together out of necessity. Meals were eaten together and fields and livestock were tended together. A drought-breaking rain was good news for everyone; an epidemic in the season's calves was a shared disaster. Families celebrated together because of a lack of alternatives if for no other reason.

Our children grow up under totally different circumstances. As soon as they enter kindergarten, they start celebrating birthdays, Christmas and Groundhog Day with their friends. Peer influence is so strong in the teen-age years partly because young people spend most of their waking hours with people their own age.

This reality makes homemaking even more important. The shared home life which in the past happened by chance must now happen by choice. An employed mother writing in *Vogue* recently declared that her children neither needed nor wanted her to be home when they arrived from school. A mother ready with cookies and a listening ear isn't necessary because today's children prefer to get their support from friends, according to this author. But if we hope that our children will be able to withstand peer pressure when necessary, we cannot afford to allow our children to get so much of their support from their friends.

Every Christian family has a responsibility to provide a community where our love for God guides our decisions. Full-time homemakers are not indispensable to a healthy Christian family, but because we invest ourselves more completely at home we have the potential of making the home a more powerful element in our ongoing struggle to follow God's path.

Witness

Our commitment to home is a witness to others of the importance we attach to family. Ever since I was a child I have been moved by the famous sculpture depicting four Marines struggling to plant the American flag on Iwo Jima. Why were those young men risking their lives for a scrap of fabric? A flag is simply a cloth with a set design; often it has very little value in terms of workmanship or materials. But flags are powerful symbols, and battles are sometimes won because a soldier, perhaps at the cost of his life, has held the flag aloft to inspire those that followed.

Our families are not scraps of fabric. They have enormous worth, but their importance is not always recognized. Competent, intelligent, gifted women who spend years of their lives at home say to the world, "My family is precious. Roots are vital. Home is important."

As Christians, our witness goes beyond this. We witness not only to the beauty of the family, but also to the special dimension that God's love brings to our lives.

Our homes have a power to witness which we as individuals do not possess. It is a wonderful thing to discover a new friend, but to stumble on a whole circle of friends can transform a life. A pastor may be a gifted preacher, but his power to convert is magnified if people who hear him can also see Christian community in action in his parish. We can affect other people by our friendship, by listening to them and talking about our own experience. But if we not only talk about our goals but also invite them to see those ideals lived out in our homes, the potential for change is much greater.

We change for many reasons. Sometimes we acquire new knowledge and are convinced to change, sometimes we are forced to change, and sometimes we are inspired to change. A real home has a tremendous power to inspire. A place where people enjoy one another, share special moments together, where their environment is in tune with their lives attracts and influences other people. Families do not necessarily need full-time homemakers to have these qualities, but a family in which one person is dedicated to homemaking will be more centered at home, and the home's power to witness will be greater.

Hospitality

The means by which homemakers expand our influence is through practicing the virtue of hospitality. Hospitality was one of the hallmarks of the early Christian communities, but today we consider it a skill rather than a virtue.

Jesus told us,

"When you give a lunch or a dinner, do not ask your friends, brothers, relations or rich neighbors, for fear they repay your courtesy by inviting you in return. No; when you have a party, invite the poor, the crippled, the lame, the blind; that they cannot pay you back means that you are fortunate, because repayment will be made to you when the virtuous rise again" (Lk 14:12-14).

Opening our homes to the poor is a potent means of allowing God to touch others through us. There are many kinds of poor: the financially poor, the physically or mentally handicapped, refugees, the emotionally damaged, and young people who are searching. Each vocation has its particular virtues, and hospitality is a virtue particularly appropriate to homemakers.

A Rose Is a Rose . . .

Even without an outreach a Christian home is beautiful in and of itself. Truth and beauty please God wherever they are found. God created macaws, those brilliantly colored birds which live deep in Amazon jungles seldom penetrated by people. There are billions of splendid stars in the universe which no one will ever see with even the most powerful telescope. Apparently God creates them for the sheer joy of it. He also delights in our homes if they are places of inner beauty, of wholeness—places where he resides.

In some important ways homes resemble

monasteries, and we can rest a little more securely in our role if we see our similarities with their long and venerable history. Monasteries have encountered their share of misunderstanding, the most common challenge being "Why would gifted people bury themselves and their talents?" (Sounds somehow familiar.) Monasteries and homes both have as their ultimate purpose the creation of a place where people can live as closely as possible with God. People question whether monasteries have an impact on society, but it was the monasteries that saved Western civilization during the Dark Ages. Contemplatives have profoundly influenced the thinking of many generations. Similarly, homemakers' influence may not be obvious, but it is profound.

It's interesting to note that monastic life has always included manual labor. Contemplative orders tune their lives very carefully to open them up to God, and the same sort of work that homemakers do has always been a part of that lifestyle. Contemplatives balance work, study and prayer, with a little time set aside for recreation. The balance of our lives is very different from a monk's, but the components of their lives are the same as ours.

Transitions

Homemakers number in the millions, and we cannot be lumped together. The mother of preschoolers has a very different life from a homemaker with teen-age children, whose days are different from the woman whose children are rapidly leaving home. Homemaking is a job which passes through several fairly predictable but very diverse stages. Roughly they break down to:

1) *The initial adjustment*—This generally coincides with the birth of a baby, and sleepless nights and perhaps the loss of an income add to the stress of coping with a drastic change in life.

2) *The preschool years*—Most of our time at this stage seems to be spent picking up shredded paper and fishing shoes out of diaper pails.

3) *Grade school*—This is perhaps the easiest stage. Our children can dress, feed and potty themselves, but they still like us and we have solid control over their activities.

4) *Junior high and high school*—At this stage our children leap toward in-dependence yet experience over-whelming peer pressure. This is a frightening time when conflicts with our children fuel our fears about them leaving us and our values behind.

5) *The emptying nest*—This is when we learn whether we balanced our invest-ment well. If we invested too heavily at home, we will be devastated when our children leave. Or, worse, they may never leave. If we invested too little, or

invested wrongly, our children may
leave with just a perfunctory nod as
they go.

The times of greatest stress for homemakers are
usually the transitions from one stage to another,
primarily into stage one and during stage five.

Years ago women went through these crises with
all their friends. Women married young, had babies a
year after they married, and the stage was set for the
next 25 years. Now some women have their first
babies in their teens and others choose to wait until
their 40s. Not only do we have the diversity of the
various stages in homemaking, we now have added
that the women experiencing each stage are a much
more diverse group than formerly.

Women who have chosen to stay home with
their preschool children generally begin to wonder
about an outside job when their children start school.
If we see our role primarily as communicating with
our children, then it seems silly for us to be home
when they are not. But if as homemakers our task is
creating a special place and special moments, and if
our power to do so comes from investing ourselves at
home, then there is no need for us to seek another
job. To be healthy, we will not invest ourselves at
home when our children are teen-agers in the same
way that we did when they were infants. We will
gradually take on more outside activities or will invite
more activities into our homes as our children get
older. But throughout the five stages of homemaking

we have important work, work which requires our time and our energy.

Sigmund Freud said that the keys to a happy life are love and work. If we rest assured of God's love and are willing to risk ourselves in building a place of love at home, then our work lies before us. And some day, after our work has been completed and we are at last coming home to stay, we will be greeted with the words, "Well done, good and faithful servant. . . . Come and join in your master's happiness" (Mt 25:21).